A
DASH OF LOVE

A COLLECTION OF JOAN RYAN'S
FAVORITE RECIPES GATHERED
OVER THE YEARS FROM
FRIENDS AND FAMILY

This book was published by Joan Ryan

SHARED PEN Edition.

www.SharedPen.com

This book is dedicated to the beloved Elizabeth "Gram" Burke who made Christmas cookies and donuts, and many other sweets to keep all of her five grandchildren happy and content.

1898—1982

INDEX

APPETIZERS AND COCKTAILS

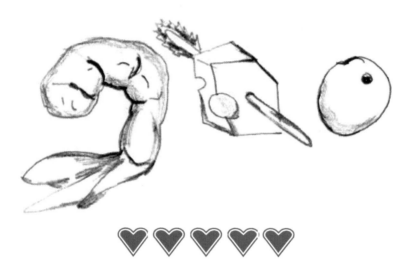

"Small cheer and great welcome makes a merry feast."
—William Shakespeare

- ♥ CAJUN SHRIMP WITH REMOULADE SAUCE

- ♥ PERFECT BOILED SHRIMP WITH DIPPING SAUCES

- ♥ FAMOUS QUESO DIP

- ♥ SHRIMP CEVICHE WITH CHIPS

- ♥ GRILLED SHISHITO PEPPERS

- ♥ ROSY HUGENER'S FAMOUS GUACAMOLE

- ♥ SMOKED SALMON APPETIZER

- ♥ TEQUILA SUNRISE COCKTAIL

- ♥ CLASSIC MANHATTAN COCKTAIL

CAJUN SHRIMP WITH REMOULADE SAUCE

Remoulade Sauce

½ cup light or regular mayonnaise

1 tablespoon minced fresh parsley leaves

2 tablespoons ketchup

2 tablespoons minced celery

1 tablespoon Dijon Mustard with seeds

2 teaspoons lemon juice

½ teaspoon Cajun seasoning

1 green onion, minced

Cajun Shrimp

1 tablespoon Cajun seasoning

1 tablespoon minced fresh parsley leaves

1 tablespoon olive oil

2 teaspoons grated fresh lemon peel

1-1/4 lb. large shrimp, shelled and deveined, with tails

Green onion and lemon peel slivers for garnish

Lemon wedges for garnish

1. In small bowl, mix all sauce ingredients. Cover and refrigerate up to 3 days if not serving right away. Makes about 1 cup.

2. In bowl, mix Cajun seasoning, oil and lemon peel. Add shrimp to spice mixture and toss until evenly coated. Place shrimp on hot grill rack over medium high heat and cook 3-4 minutes or until shrimp are opaque throughout turning shrimp only once.

3. Transfer shrimp to platter. Serve with lemon wedges and sauce. May be served at room temperature and made a couple hours ahead.

   Makes 10 to 12 appetizer portions

A FOUR STAR FAVORITE

I found this recipe many years ago in Bon Appetite magazine. The recipe is now wrinkled and stained from having prepared it so many times. This is a refreshing change from the traditional boiled shrimp with cocktail sauce and only a little more effort to prepare. Your guests will love you!

Here's my good friend Kathy Fanning holding prepared Cajun Shrimp. Kathy is an outstanding cook and loves to entertain. We have exchanged many recipes since we first met in our twenties when we worked together at American Hospital Supply Corporation.

PERFECT BOILED SHRIMP WITH DIPPING SAUCES

Shrimp

1 pound shrimp (no matter the size of shrimp)

1/4 cup cider vinegar

4 tablespoons Old Bay Seasoning, to taste

Spices if desired

Joe's Stone Crab Mustard Sauce

1 tablespoon + 1/2 teaspoon Coleman's dry mustard

1 cup mayonnaise

2 teaspoons Worcestershire sauce

1 teaspoon A-1 Steak sauce

1 teaspoon heavy cream

1 tablespoon milk

Salt

Dijon Sambal Aioli

3/4 cup mayonnaise

2 tablespoons Siricha hot sauce

1 tablespoon Dijon mustard

Pinch of salt

1 tablespoon diced chives

1. Fill a pot with enough water to cover the shrimp plus 1-2 inches beyond. Cook shrimp over medium high heat while constantly stirring. Don't worry about the water boiling or time elapsed as it does not matter! When you see 1 or 2 shrimp float then drain immediately and have an ice bath waiting, to shock the shrimp and stop cooking process.

2. Mustard Sauce: Place the mustard in a mixing bowl or bowl of an electric mixer. Add the mayonnaise and beat for 1 minute. Add the Worcestershire sauce, steak sauce, cream, milk and a pinch of salt. Beat until mixture is well blended and creamy. Chill until ready to serve.

3. Dijon Sambal Aioli. Mix together ingredients. Chill until ready to serve.

   Makes 10 to 12 appetizer portions

BOILED SHRIMP DOESN'T HAVE TO BE BORING

You would think that boiling shrimp would be simple, but having done it wrong so many times, I was happy to find this recipe for perfect boiled shrimp. Of course, you can always buy prepared cooked shrimp and serve that too!

The mustard sauce, like the name says, is the one served at Joe's Stone Crab in Miami (and Chicago). Not only does it work well with cold shrimp and crab, it is also a terrific accompaniment to grilled pork tenderloin or on sandwiches.

The Dijon Sambal Aioli has a kick and is also very versatile, but definitely delicious with shrimp.

Joan Delott is displaying perfect boiled shrimp. Shrimp is a mainstay appetizer when Joan entertains. Joan, a good friend, was my neighbor in Long Grove, IL. Most recently, Joan and husband Steve are spending the winter in San Diego, which we love!

FAMOUS QUESO DIP

1 lb. Velveeta cheese, cut into cubes
1 can (10 oz.) RO*TEL Diced Tomatoes and Green Chilies, not drained
Tortilla chips

1. Combine cheese and RO*TEL ingredients in a microwavable bowl.

2. Microwave on high for 5 minutes or until Velveeta is completely melted and mixture is well blended, stirring after 3 minutes.

3. Serve with tortilla chips.

   Makes 24 2-tablespoon appetizer portions

CAUTION: THIS DIP CAN BE ADDICTIVE

Growing up, our family (a.k.a., the Martin People) would not think of having appetizers without also serving what we called "Rotel." Back in the '70s Rotel diced tomatoes were not available in Chicago, so our neighbors used to "import" Rotel from Oklahoma for us.

Today Ro*Tel is available in most grocery stores. Whenever I serve this dip, everyone always loves it, even those health conscious folks who otherwise would not dream of eating Velveeta! Just don't answer them when they ask for the ingredients.

Famous Queso Dip

SHRIMP CEVICHE WITH CHIPS

4 limes
2 pounds of medium shrimp
¼ cup (about 3 limes total) freshly squeezed lime juice
6 scallions trimmed and finely chopped
2-4 Serrano chilies finely chopped
¼ cup cider vinegar
2 teaspoons finely chopped fresh thyme
1 teaspoon dried oregano, preferably Mexican
2 large ripe avocados, peeled, pitted and diced
¼ cup finely chopped fresh cilantro
2 teaspoons salt
Tortilla chips for serving

1. Fill a large pot with 1 quart water. Cut 4 limes in half, squeeze their juice into pot; add lime halves. Bring to a boil, then turn off heat; let mixture steep about 10 minutes. Return to boil.

2. Add shrimp to pot. As soon as water returns to a rolling boil, pour shrimp mixture into a colander; discard cooking liquid and limes. Return shrimp to pot; cover; and let stand for 15 minutes. Transfer shrimp to a baking sheet and spread them out. Let stand until cool enough to handle.

3. Peel and devein shrimp, and cut into thirds. Transfer to a medium bowl; stir in 1/4 cup lime juice and the scallions, chilies, vinegar, thyme, and oregano. Let stand at room temperature 1 hour, stirring occasionally.

4. When ready to serve, stir avocados, cilantro, and salt into shrimp mixture. Serve with tortilla chips.

Makes 8-10 appetizer portions

FABULOUS CEVICHE!

I had this shrimp ceviche for the first time at Lisa and Tim Bridgeman's beautiful home in Solana Beach. Lisa is an outstanding cook.

While this is technically called Ceviche, the shrimp are actually boiled rather than "cooked" in lime juice like traditional Ceviche. For those who don't like traditional Ceviche, I guarantee that you will like this!

Shrimp Ceviche

GRILLED SHISHITO PEPPERS

1 pound Shishito peppers, washed and thoroughly dried
Canola Oil
2 tablespoon Ponzu oil (a.k.a, Kikkoman Japanese citrus oil)

1. In a medium sauté pan, heat canola oil over medium to medium high heat or toss the peppers in canola oil and heat on an indoor or outdoor grill.

2. Add Shishitu peppers and sauté or grill till browned and softened (6 – 8 minutes).

3. Pour Ponzu oil over cooked peppers to lightly coat each one.

Makes 8-10 appetizer portions

EASY TO MAKE AND HEALTHY TOO

Shishito peppers are the Japanese cousin to Spain's famed Padrón peppers. Delicately sweet and usually mild, they are an easy snack to throw on the grill or cook in a sauté pan or grill pan.

This recipe came from Terry and Debbie Mathew who first tasted these peppers in a restaurant and asked the chef for the recipe. This is an unusual appetizer which most people haven't tasted before, and is always a hit!

Here's Sharon Taylor who taste-tested the grilled Shishito peppers recipe for me. Sharon is an awesome golfer, bridge player and cook who I first met in Chicago and who now lives in Fort Meyers, Florida with her husband Barry.

ROSY HUGENER'S FAMOUS GUACAMOLE

6 big avocados, mashed
Juice of 3 limes
3 finely chopped Serrano peppers
1 white onion, finely chopped
1 bunch cilantro leave, finely chopped
1-2 tablespoons salt or to taste

1. Mix all ingredients by hand until blended. Do not use food processer or beaters to mix.

2. Serve immediately with chips or as accompaniment to tacos or other Mexican fare.

   Makes 15-20 appetizer portions

THIS IS THE BEST GUACAMOLE

Rosy Hugener, who grew up in Mexico City but now lives in Long Grove, IL always serves her famous guacamole whenever she entertains. Although Rosy makes it from memory with no formal recipe, I finally got her explain the recipe to me and have made it ever since to rave reviews.

It is very typical that when I ask a hostess, "What can I bring when we come to your house for dinner," that she answers "Rosy's Guacamole!"

Here's Rosy Hugener with her famous guacamole in hand. Rosy is an accomplished business woman, and owner of "Shared Pen" publishing company. She is my publisher for this book. Rosy is also an outstanding tennis player, is the mother of two wonderful and very smart children, and I love talking to her because she is so interesting and well read.

SMOKED SALMON APPETIZER

2 pound whole side of smoked salmon
1/2 cup of good mayonnaise or Veganaise
1-2 tablespoons of prepared horseradish
Capers
Lemon slices
Arugula
Crackers or flatbread

1. Mix horseradish and mayonnaise to make a sauce for the salmon and place in small bowl.

2. Arrange salmon on a plate with bowl of horseradish sauce and arugula and lemon slices. Garnish salmon with capers.

   Makes 15-20 appetizer portions

FRESH AND LIGHT

Jacquie brought this fabulous appetizer to our home at our pool party a couple of years ago. I have since served this often and take credit for it as my own. :)

Here's the beautiful and intelligent Jacquie Powers, along with a picture of her smoked salmon appetizer. Jacquie lives in Olivenhein, CA with her husband Curtis and her two wonderful children. Jacquie grew up in New York and is now a big surfer girl, steel drum player and swimmer. Jacquie is a retired teacher of middle school mathematics.

TEQUILA SUNRISE

2 ounces tequila
4 ounces orange juice
1/2 ounce grenadine
Orange slice for garnish
Maraschino cherry for garnish

1. Pour the tequila and the orange juice into a highball glass with ice cubes. Stir.

2. Slowly pour the grenadine around the inside edge of the glass, it will sink slowly and mix with the other ingredients naturally.

3. Garnish with the orange slice and cherry

Makes one cocktail

IT'S ANOTHER
TEQUILA SUNRISE
STARIN' SLOWLY
CROSS THE SKY

—THE EAGLES

Here is the studly Jack Egofske, my nephew, along with his favorite "go to" cocktail — the Tequila Sunrise. Jack attends Miami University of Ohio, is a "frat boy" and possible accounting major (like me — his favorite aunt). Jack grew up in Evanston, IL where he was a hockey and football star. When he was a little boy he dressed in costume ever day. Jack is his own person and a riot to be around which is why he has so many friends!

CLASSIC MANHATTAN COCKTAIL

Ice
2 parts whisky
1 part sweet vermouth
1 to 2 dashes bitters, such as Angostura (optional)
Pimento or blue cheese stuffed olives

1. Place ice in a cocktail shaker. Add the whiskey, vermouth and bitters.

2. Add 1 to two stuffed olives and enjoy.

    Makes one cocktail

GEORGE'S SIGNATURE COCKTAIL

George drinks his Manhattan every evening and loves it with pimento or blue cheese olives, rather than the traditional cherries. When he came to our house in California a few years ago during "cutie" tangerine season, George picked the "cuties" off our tree and then deemed it Tangerine Tuesday! We served tangerines in our salad that night and with our chicken, and George even put a few in his Manhattan.

Here is George Egofske, my wonderful step-father who has been married to my mother for over ten years, along with a picture of his favorite cocktail, the classic Manhattan. George is the father of seven terrific children who I count as my friends and relatives too, A.K.A the "step people." George served as the beloved athletic director of Rich South High School for many years where he made a positive difference for so many students and athletes. George is an avid golfer too. We love having George as part of the "Martin people."

SOUPS AND SANDWICHES

"To make a good pot of soup, the pot must only simmer or smile."
—French Proverb

- ♥ BROCCOLI WATERCRESS SOUP

- ♥ CHICKEN, SHRIMP AND ANDOUILLE SAUSAGE GUMBO

- ♥ CHILI CON CARNE

- ♥ LOBSTER BISQUE

- ♥ ANGELA'S CHILI BLANCO

- ♥ GREEK AVGOLEMONO SOUP

- ♥ MARSHALL FIELD'S SPECIAL TURKEY SANDWICH

- ♥ PEANUT BUTTER AND JELLY PANINI

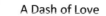

BROCCOLI WATERCRESS SOUP

3 medium leeks
1 teaspoon cider vinegar
1 cup (2 sticks) unsalted butter
1 medium yellow onion, coarsely chopped
1 tablespoon salt
1 teaspoon freshly ground black pepper
2 quarts chicken stock or canned broth
2 medium all-purpose potatoes, peeled and sliced
2 bunches broccoli
2 bunches watercress, stems removed, rinsed, patted dry
1/2 cups heavy or whipping cream

1. Cut the green tops and root ends from the leeks and discard. Cut the leeks lengthwise in half and soak in cold water mixed with the vinegar, to cover, for 15 minutes Rinse, pat dry, and coarsely chop.

2. Melt the butter in a stock pot over very low heat. Add the leeks, onion, salt and pepper and cook until the vegetables are limp, about 15 minutes.

3. Add the stock and potatoes and simmer uncovered for 15 minutes.

4. Trim the ends of the broccoli stalks and discard. Slice the stalks. Measure and reserve 1 cup florets. Add the remaining florets with the sliced stalks tot the soup and simmer for 10 minutes. Remove from the heat, stir in the watercress, and let stand for 2 minutes.

5. Process the soup in small batches in a food processor fitted with a steel blade or in a blender, then pass through a food mill. (You can skip this step, soup will just be crunchier). Whisk in the cream in a slow stream. Warm the soup over low heat.

6. Blanch the reserved florets in boiling water for 1 minute. Ladle the soup into serving bowls and garnish with the reserved florets

8 to 10 portions

SOUP IS COMFORT

This is a pale green soup of mild leeks, peppery watercress and crunchy broccoli. Potatoes and heavy cream give the soup a smooth, satisfying texture, while blanched broccoli florets lend a crisp contrast.

I have making this soup for many years. It makes a great first course to your special dinner party, or works well as an entrée with crusty bread and a salad for your family. This is a favorite of my daughter Kelly.

Broccoli Watercress Soup

♥ A Dash of Love

CHICKEN, SHRIMP AND ANDOUILLE SAUSAGE GUMBO

Roux
1 cup of butter
1 1/4 cup of flour

Gumbo
2 tablespoons file powder (purchased in spice section of grocery store)
3 quarts chicken broth or stock
2 cups of canned tomatoes
2 pounds of frozen sliced okra
2 tablespoons olive oil
24 ounces of chicken breast from purchased rotisserie chicken, diced
4 cups diced onions
1 tablespoon minced garlic
2 cups celery
1 cup scallion (sliced, green and white parts)
1 cup chopped fresh flat leaf Italian parsley
2 cups seeded/diced green bell peppers
1 pound Andouille sausage (or smoked pork sausage, sliced)
1 lb. uncooked med/large shrimp, peeled, deveined and tails removed
2 teaspoons dried oregano
1 teaspoon dried basil
1 teaspoon dried thyme
1 tablespoon Old Bay Seasoning
2 tablespoons Cajun seasoning

Roux
1. Melt the butter in a s sauté pan, stir in the flour and turn down the heat to medium. Cook for four minutes, stirring constantly with a wooden spoon until the mixture has the consistency of wet sand and the aroma of toasted nuts (this stage is a "blonde roux").
2. Continue cooking and stirring for 15 minutes longer, until the roux is a deep mahogany color; take care not to burn the roux.
3. Remove the pan from heat and transfer roux to a bowl. Set aside to cool.

Gumbo
1. Pour 2 tablespoons of oil into a large, heavy bottomed sauce pan and set over medium-high heat. Add onion, garlic, celery and bell peppers and sauté for 2-3 minutes until onions are translucent, stirring often. Add the sausage and sauté for two minutes longer.
2. Add basil, thyme, Old Bay Seasoning, oregano, Cajun seasoning and file powder and sauté for one minute, stirring often.
3. Add the chicken broth, tomatoes, okra, shrimp and the reserved diced chicken and bring to a boil. Turn down the heat to medium-low and bring the soup to a simmer. Add the brown roux while stirring until it is well incorporated and the soup begins to thicken.
4. Turn down the heat to low and simmer, covered for an hour. Stir in the scallions and parsley. Season with salt and pepper to taste.

Makes 6 to 8 entrée portions (about 3 quarts)

GUMBO MUMBO

Gumbo may have originated in the Creole cuisine in New Orleans, but it's a soup that entered the American mainstream. Gumbos, like many other Creole and Cajun recipes, are based on a brown roux—a thickened mixture of flour and butter—and contain distinctive ingredients such as okra, chicken, spicy sausage, tomatoes and file powder (ground sassafras leaves).

Although the ingredient list is long, this soup is actually simple and not too time consuming to make. I serve this Gumbo over about a 1/3 cup rice into each soup bowl.

I ate this for the first time at the Zodiac Room in Neiman Marcus, and the recipe comes from their cookbook.

Chicken, Shrimp and Andouille Sausage Gumbo

CHILI CON CARNE

1 pound lean, lean ground beef – 5% fat max

1 15 ounce can black beans, drained

15 ounce can tomato sauce

4 cups vegetable broth

1 bunch cilantro, chopped

1 Serrano or jalapeno pepper, minced

1 large onion chopped.

6-7 cloves garlic (the more the better)

1 tablespoon Chili powder

2 teaspoon Italian seasoning

2 pinch Cayenne pepper (optional)

2 teaspoon Emeril's Original Essence (i.e., can be found in the spice aisle)

Salt to taste

1. Brown ground beef, remove from pan and drain.

2. Sauté onion and garlic until soft.

3. Add cooked beef and all ingredients except beans and cilantro.

4. Bring to boil and simmer for 15 minutes.

5. Add beans and cilantro and cook for 5 more minutes.

   4 to 6 entrée portions (about 1.5 quarts)

CHILE MADE LIGHT

I adapted this recipe from a diet cookbook, later adding in cilantro and serrano peppers for added flavor. I make this chili often in a large batch and then eat this for lunch on the run. It is satisfying and yet light in fat and calories.

The ladies from Royal Melbourne (our former neighborhood in Long Grove, Illinois) tested many of the recipes for this cookbook and brought them to Joan Delott's Oscar party in March 2014. Here is the beautiful Teresa Brandt displaying the chili recipe that she prepared in her "test kitchen." Teresa is a "Jersey Girl" who loves to laugh and is always fun and optimistic and up for anything! She has two beautiful daughters just like their mother.

LOBSTER BISQUE

½ cup dry white wine

⅛ teaspoon celery salt

⅛ teaspoon onion powder

⅛ teaspoon garlic powder

⅛ teaspoon white pepper

1½ tablespoons all-purpose flour

½ cup water

1½ tablespoons Better Than Bouillon® Lobster Base (available near the soup or spice aisle in the grocery store)

3 tablespoons tomato paste

2 cups half-and-half

1. In a large saucepan, add wine. Cook over medium-high heat until wine is reduced by half.

2. In a small bowl, combine celery salt, onion powder, garlic powder, pepper and flour, set aside.

3. Add water to reduced wine, lower heat to medium-low.

4. Whisk in Lobster Base and tomato paste.

5. Add set aside dry-ingredients and whisk until smooth.

6. Gradually add half-and-half while continually whisking. Cook until bisque thickens, about 10 minutes, stirring occasionally.

7. After adding half-and-half, add ½ cup finely chopped, cooked lobster meat. (shrimp or crab can be substituted.)

2 portions

ELEGANT AND FOOL PROOF

I often ordered Lobster bisque when dining out because it is so delicious but I never eat it at home. But then I found this recipe on line and it is so easy that I can make it anytime. You can double or triple the recipe of course to serve at a dinner party as a starter. You will bowl over your guests!

The ladies from Royal Melbourne (our former neighborhood in Long Grove, Illinois) tested many of the recipes for this cookbook and brought them to Joan Delott's Oscar party in March 2014.

Here is Maureen Sexton displaying the Lobster Bisque recipe that she prepared in her "test kitchen." Not only is Maureen a beautiful person inside and out, Maureen is a marathon runner (she's done "Boston"), a mother and awesome business woman.

ANGELA'S CHILI BLANCO

1 16 ounce can Great Northern Beans, drained

1/2 of 16 ounce jar Mrs. Renfro's Green Salsa

3 cups chicken broth

Salt to taste

2 cups grated Monterey Jack cheese

Breast of chicken from purchased rotisserie chicken, shredded (i.e., homemade cooked chicken or white meat canned chicken can be used as well)

Diced tomatoes, additional grated cheese, chopped scallions and chopped cilantro for garnish

1. Combine, salsa, chicken broth, and beans. Heat to boiling.

2. Before serving, add shredded chicken and cheese. Stir until cheese is melted and chicken is heated through.

3. Salt to taste. Add more salsa to increase "heat" if desired.

4. Garnish, if desired, with diced tomatoes, additional grated cheese, chopped scallions and chopped cilantro for garnish.

Makes 4-6 portions

GREAT FOR A FOOTBALL PARTY

Angela Kent brought this Chicken Chili in a slow cooker to our Super Bowl party. Our team didn't win, but the chili was a huge hit. I make this often as a one dish dinner or a quick microwave lunch.

Here's Angela Kent with her prepared Chili Blanco. Not only is Angela beautiful and smart, she is a terrific cook and mother of two smart and athletic boys. I met Angela when I first moved to San Diego and we have been friends ever since. I sent her an email afterward with the subject line: "Where have you have been all my life?" Needless to say, we are kindred spirits.

GREEK AVGOLEMONO SOUP

GOOD FOR THE SOUL

Avgolemono soup is a Greek specialty that Lorraine Surnamer learned to cook from her grandmother. Avgolemono is a Greek word — avgo means egg and lemono means lemon.

The tartness of the lemon and savory taste of chicken marry together to make a fresh and bright tasting yet hearty soup.

Prepared roasted rotisserie chicken

2 or 3 celery stalks cleaned, cut in 1/4 inch slices

1 cup carrots, cut in 1/4 inch slices

1/2 cup lemon juice

1 teaspoon each of sage, parsley, thyme to taste

1/2 teaspoon salt, to taste

4 quarts water

2-3 cubes of chicken bouillon or to taste

2 cups precooked orzo or rice

3 eggs beaten

1. Chop up chicken into bite sized pieces. Reserve bones and skin.

2. Bring water to a boil. Add chicken bones and skin, chopped onion, celery, carrots, and bouillon. Boil chicken bones, bouillon, and veggies for 30 minutes. Remove bones.

3. Whip lemon juice and eggs with egg beater till frothy. If broth is cooked, take a small bowl with lemon juice mixture, add broth slowly, mix with beaten eggs, stirring in one direction only so that eggs do not curdle. Keep adding a cup or so at a time broth into lemon juice mixture.

4. Add lemon juice mixture back into soup, again stirring in the same direction slowly. Add in chicken pieces, veggies, and herbs.

5. May serve with crusty bread. Store in refrigerator.

Here's Lorraine Surnamer and a picture of a bowl of her Avgolemono soup. Lorraine lives in Del Mar, CA and has two lovely daughters. Lorraine is a retired senior executive from Qualcomm and now is able to enjoy hiking, tennis and being with friends and family. Lorraine is a serious scrabble player who beats me handily! She is a generous and wonderful friend.

MARSHALL FIELD'S SPECIAL TURKEY SANDWICH

Open-Faced Sandwich

1/2 fresh crispy head iceberg lettuce

3 -5 slices of freshly roasted turkey breast (white meat only)

1/4 to 1/2 cup thousand island dressing (i.e., per recipe below or using a good purchased dressing)

1 slice aged Swiss cheese, thinly sliced

1 slice rye bread

1 teaspoon butter, softened

2 slices bacon, cooked

1 slice hard-boiled egg

1 slice tomato

Thousand Island Dressing

1 cup mayonnaise

1/2 cup Heinz Chili Sauce

2 tablespoons sweet pickle relish

2 large green olives, pitted and finely chopped

1/2 teaspoon dried tarragon

1 dash Tabasco sauce

1 dash Worcestershire sauce

1 hard-boiled egg, finely chopped (optional)

salt, to taste

1. Butter rye bread and place on a large cold serving plate. Cover bread with Swiss cheese slice, followed by one or two slices of turkey. Take a nice large outer lettuce leaf from the head of iceberg and set aside. Slice the iceberg lettuce in a few large sections and arrange a section on top of the turkey and Swiss cheese.

2. Combine all Thousand Island Dressing ingredients. Refrigerate at least 30 minutes. Yields one and three-fourths cups dressing or enough for about 6 sandwiches.

3. Cover the open-face sandwich with a big lettuce leaf. Top with several slices of turkey. Pour a very ample amount of dressing over the lettuce, allowing it to puddle slightly all around the plate. Place the bacon in an X across the sandwich. Place tomato slice and egg slice atop mound with parsley sprig. Garnish with a large stuffed green olive. Serve immediately.

Makes one sandwich.

STRAIGHT FROM THE WALNUT ROOM AT MARSHALL FIELDS

Having grown up in Chicago, it was always a special treat to have lunch at the Walnut Room at the Marshall Field's department store on State Street, especially at Christmas. We always ordered the signature open faced turkey sandwich.

While "Field's" has since closed, we can still make that special turkey sandwich, which works well using left-over Thanksgiving turkey.

Marshall Field's Special Turkey Sandwich

PEANUT BUTTER AND JELLY PANINI

4 slices cinnamon bread or walnut bread about 1/2 inch thick

1 tablespoon unsalted butter at room temperature

4 tablespoons smooth or chunky peanut butter

2 tablespoons jam or preserves

1. Preheat the sandwich panini grill. Place the bread slices on a work surface and spread one side of each with the butter. Turn and spread the unbuttered sides with the peanut butter, dividing it evenly, then spread the jam over the peanut butter on two of the slides. Place the remaining two bread slides on top, peanut butter side down, and press to pack gently.

2. Place the panini sandwich in the grill, close the top plate, and cook until the bread is golden and toasted, and the peanut butter is warmed and beginning to melt, about 2 to 4 minutes. Cut each sandwich in half and serve right away.

   Makes two sandwiches

UPSCALE PB&J

When our son Pete was a child, he had a limited list of acceptable menu items. He would only eat chicken tenders, spaghetti-Os, Kraft macaroni and cheese and PB&J. Pete is now grown and has a much expanded palate. He received a Panini grill as a gift a few years ago and discovered that his old favorite — the PB&J sandwich — could be made as a Panini. Voila!

Grilling the bread and warming the peanut butter intensifies the flavor of both this upscale peanut butter and jelly sandwich. Try artisan-crafted jams and preserves, such as morello cherry or mixed berry. A good-quality raspberry jelly will work just fine too.

Here's our handsome and talented son, Pete Ryan along with his favorite PB&J Panini sandwich. Pete lives and works in San Francisco where he has lived since he graduated from college. He held sales positions at Oracle, LinkedIn and the start up DoubleDutch. These days Peter is working on creating his own company — GoGo Hire. John and I are so proud of the man he has become.

SALADS

"If you think you are a mushroom, jump into the basket."
—Russian Proverb

- ♥ BROCCOLI SALAD

- ♥ JOANNE'S ASPARAGAS AND BLUE CHEESE SALAD

- ♥ LUXEMBOURG SALAD

- ♥ ASIAN COLESLAW WITH CHICKEN

- ♥ TUNA NICOISE SALAD

- ♥ CURRIED CHICKEN SALAD WITH TOASTED ALMONDS AND MIXED GREENS

- ♥ CHICKEN SALAD WITH PESTO MAYONNAISE

- ♥ SPAGHETTI SALAD

- ♥ CLASSIC DELI TUNA SALAD

BROCCOLI SALAD

2 heads fresh broccoli
1 red onion
1/2 pound bacon
3/4 cup raisins, craisins, or dried cherries
3/4 cup sliced almonds or honey roasted cashews
1 cup mayonnaise
1/2 cup white sugar
2 tablespoons white wine vinegar

1. Place bacon in a deep skillet and cook over medium high heat until evenly brown. Cool and crumble.

2. Cut the broccoli into bite-size pieces and cut the onion into thin bite-size slices. Combine with the bacon, raisins, your nuts and mix well.

3. To prepare the dressing, mix the mayonnaise, sugar and vinegar together until smooth. Stir into the salad, let chill and serve.

Makes 6 to 8 portions

THE PERFECT SIDE SALAD

I first ate this salad back in the eighties at one of Kathy Fanning's legendary dinner parties, which she held at their first home in Arlington Heights, Illinois. I have made it often ever since. It is works well at a dinner party or a casual barbecue...it is very versatile. This salad is always a hit, easy to make and the broccoli makes it semi-healthy!

Broccoli Salad

JOANNE'S ASPARAGUS AND BLUE CHEESE SALAD

Asparagus
2 bunches asparagus spears or baby asparagus
Course salt and pepper
Olive oil

Balsamic Dressing
2 tablespoons balsamic vinegar
¾ cup olive oil
1 teaspoon salt
1 teaspoon pepper
½ teaspoon sugar
1 tablespoon parsley
10 ripe plum tomatoes
1 cup crumbled blue cheese

1. To prepare the asparagus, cut spears in half lengthwise. Place on cookie sheet; drizzle with olive oil, coarse salt and cracked pepper. Bake at 350 degrees until al dente.

2. Mix all dressing ingredients and set aside. Best if made one day in advance.

3. Core and remove seeds from tomatoes and prepare ½ inch dice.

4. On large oval platter, line each side with asparagus spears. Place blue cheese in the center of the platter, the line up the asparagus spears on each side of the platter. Place the diced tomatoes around the blue cheese and overlapping onto the rows of asparagus spears.

5. Drizzle dressing over entire salad.

   Makes 8 to 10 portions

THIS SALAD IS TASTY AND LIGHT

Joanne Balogh and her husband Mike were included as "fillers" for our gourmet club one evening. Joanne brought this beautiful and delicious salad and everyone loved it. All of the gourmet club took her recipe and I have made it countless times since then. After that first gourmet club dinner, Joanne and Mike were formally asked to join.

This salad is perfect for a buffet dinner.

Here is my very good friend Joanne holding her famous Asparagus and Blue Cheese Salad. Joanne and I met back in the early 90s when we both worked for the NutraSweet company — she worked in sales and I worked in finance — but we nevertheless bonded. We immediately became good friends and have spent countless hours shopping, lunching, gossiping, vacationing and just hanging out together. Joanne lives in Barrington, Illinois with her husband Mike, and two wonderful and talented boys.

LUXEMBOURG SALAD

Salad

9 cups torn salad greens (a combination of leafy lettuces and chicory)

1 1/2 cups crumbled blue cheese

Croutons

2 thick slices bacon

4 slices day-old bread [French bread] cut into 1-inch squares

Luxembourg Dressing

4 cloves garlic, finely minced

1/3 cup balsamic vinegar

2 tablespoons fresh lemon juice

1 1/2 tablespoons Dijon-style mustard

1 1/2 tablespoons mixed salad herbs (parsley, chives, tarragon, and chervil)

1 cup olive oil

Salt and freshly ground black pepper, to taste

Salad and Croutons

1. Fry the bacon pieces in a medium-size skillet until crisp. Drain on paper towels and reserve the fat in the skillet.

2. Sauté the bread slowly in the hot bacon fat until crisp and browned.

3. Combine the salad greens, bacon, croutons, and blue cheese in a salad bowl.

4. Add the dressing, toss, and serve immediately.

Luxembourg Dressing

1. Whisk the garlic, vinegar, lemon juice, and mustard together in a mixing bowl. Whisk in the herbs. Gradually whisk in the oil. Season to taste with salt and pepper.

Makes 6 portions

A MEMORABLE SALAD FOR THAT SPECIAL MEAL

Leafy greens, crisp bacon lardoons, and sautéed croutons—all coated with a mustard vinaigrette.

This is a perfect accompaniment to that special holiday dinner of beef and potatoes. I made this for our gourmet club back in Chicago and it passed muster with them.

Luxembourg Salad

ASIAN COLESLAW WITH CHICKEN

1 (3 ounce) package vegetable or chicken flavor ramen noodles with seasoning packet

1 (3 ounce) package sunflower seed kernels (shelled)

1 (3 ounce) package sliced almonds

1 bunch green onions, chopped

1 cup bottled oil and vinegar salad dressing (such as Paul Newman's)

1/2 cup white sugar

1 (16 ounce) package shredded cabbage (coleslaw) - or can use shredded broccoli, and/or carrots or all three

2 grilled chicken breasts, sliced (optional)

1. Crush the ramen noodles in a bowl, and stir in the seasoning packet, sunflower seeds, almonds, green onions, oil and vinegar dressing, and sugar, mixing until the sugar is dissolved.

2. Fan out sliced grilled chicken breasts on top of salad if desired.

Serves 4

COLESLAW WITH A TWIST

My friend Sandra Rosenberg introduced me to this coleslaw recipe many years ago and I have made it often ever since.

This makes a great side dish at a barbeque or can be a lunch entrée salad with the addition of grilled chicken.

Asian Coleslaw

TUNA NICOISE SALAD

A CLASSIC FRENCH SALAD

Tuna Nicoise salad originated in France many years ago. I take great pride in making this salad with chunk albacore tuna packed in spring water, the best type of canned tuna you can buy, and it's the key to success in this recipe.

I have had this composed salad with cooked fresh tuna, but I preferred the time-tested original.

Salad

1 pound fresh green beans, trimmed
12 ounces mixed lettuce greens, washed and dried
4 cans (6 ounces each) chunk white albacore tuna, packed in water, chilled and drained
4 hard boiled eggs, cut in half lengthwise
2 vine-ripened tomatoes, each cut into 6 wedges
1 1/3 cups pitted Nicoise or Kalamata olives
2 lbs. Yukon Gold potatoes
½ cup sliced red onion.

Black Pepper Dressing

1 ¼ cups mayonnaise
¼ cup red wine vinegar
2 tablespoons freshly ground black pepper
1 teaspoon salt
Pinch of sugar
½ cup olive oil

1. Bring a saucepan of salted water to a boil over high heat and add the potatoes. Turn down the heat to medium and simmer for about 10 minutes until tender. Drain in a colander and let cool. Transfer to the refrigerator and let chill.

2. To prepare the dressing, place the mayonnaise in a mixing bowl, add the vinegar, pepper, salt, and sugar, and whisk to combine. Slowly add the oil in a steady stream, whisking constantly, until well incorporated. Transfer to an airtight container and store in the refrigerator.

3. To prepare the salad, bring a saucepan of heavily salted water to a boil, add the beans and blanch for 3 or 4 minutes until tender and bright green; do not overcook. Drain the beans and transfer to an ice bath to stop the cooking. When cold, drain the beans again and pat dry with paper towels.

4. Place the salad greens in a mixing bowl and add ½ cup of the dressing. Toss together to mix well and transfer to chilled salad plates or bowls. For each serving, artistically arrange the contents of one can of drained tuna on top of the greens and arrange two egg halves, three tomato wedges, 1/3 cup of the olives, and one quarter of the blanched green beans around the tuna. Cut the reserved chilled potatoes into ¼ inch slices, place around the salads, and top each salad with the onion slices. Pass additional dressing at the table.

Tuna Nicoise Salad

CURRIED CHICKEN SALAD WITH TOASTED ALMONDS AND MIXED GREENS

Curried Chicken Salad

2 ¾ cups poached chicken breasts (or use purchased rotisserie chicken for a short cut)

1 tablespoon cider vinegar

½ cup finely diced celery

¾ cup mayonnaise

3 tablespoons heavy cream

¼ cup mango chutney

2 teaspoons curry powder

¾ cups raisins

Creamy Mango Dressing

¾ cup mayonnaise

¼ cup mango chutney

3 tablespoons heavy cream

Mixed Greens and Almonds

12 ounces mixed lettuce greens (mesclun or spring mix), washed and dried.

1 cup toasted sliced blanched almonds

Chicken Salad

1. Place the diced chicken in a mixing bowl, sprinkle with the cider vinegar, and let sit for 10 minutes. Add the celery, mayonnaise, and cream, and then fold in the chutney, curry powder, raisins, salt, and pepper until the mixture is well combined. Transfer to an airtight container and store in the refrigerator for several hours, and preferably overnight, so that the mixture chills and the flavors can develop.

Creamy Mango Dressing

1. Place the mayonnaise, chutney and cream in a mixing bowl and whisk to combine. Reserve in the refrigerator.

2. Place the lettuce greens in a mixing bowl and toss the dressing. Transfer to chilled salad plates. Place about 1 cup of the chicken salad on top of the greens on each plate and garnish with the toasted almonds. Garnish the salad, if desired, with sliced fresh fruit such as melon and pineapple

Makes 4 to 6 portions

PERFECT FOR A SHOWER

I made this salad for the wedding shower of my niece, Laura Fox Wallis. I prepared the salad at home the day before and then transported it to my sister's home in Indianapolis where the shower took place. It got rave reviews and I have made it often ever since.

The contrasts in flavors and textures—the spiced curry, the sweet and silky dressing, the crunchy almonds and chewy raisins—are what really make this salad stand out.

Curried Chicken Salad with Toasted Almonds and Mixed Greens

CHICKEN SALAD WITH PESTO MAYONNAISE

1 1/2 lbs. chicken breast meat from purchased rotisserie chicken or prepared poached or grilled chicken

1/2 cup marinated sun-dried tomatoes

1 head butter lettuce

1/3 cup mayonnaise

3 tablespoons prepared pesto

1. Cut the chicken into one inch dice. Cut the tomatoes into thin strips. Separate the head of lettuce into leaves. Rinse and dry the lettuce.

2. Combine the mayonnaise and pesto, stirring until well blended. Then fold in the chicken and tomatoes

3. Arrange the lettuce leaves on 4 plates. Top with the chicken salad and serve.

   Makes 4 servings

5 INGREDIENTS IN 10 MINUTES

My sister Theresa made this wonderful chicken salad for daughter Kelly and me when I first visited her home in Riverside, California 20 years ago. We loved it!   I have since made this many times since then. Not only is it so easy and simple to make, you can keep the store bought sun dried tomatoes and pesto on hand to use with your left over chicken to make this beautiful salad.

Here's my beautiful and talented sister Theresa Farrell, along with her signature chicken salad. Theresa is a very successful development officer or Goodwill Industries, mother of two grown children, and outstanding soprano singer .She and her husband, travel the world with husband Jay's job as University of California professor and president of the global electrical engineering society.

SPAGHETTI SALAD

1 pound spaghetti, broken into 4 inch pieces

1 8 ounce bottle of Italian salad dressing

4 tablespoons McCormick Salad Supreme seasoning

4 – 5 cups chopped assorted vegetables (i.e., cherry tomatoes, broccoli florets, shredded carrots, sliced zucchini, chopped green pepper, chopped red onion)

1. Cook pasta according to package direction. Rinse and drain.

2. In large bowl, combine pasta, salad dressing and Salad Supreme seasoning.

3. Toss in vegetables. Cover and refrigerate until ready to serve.

Makes 12 servings

A GREAT SUMMER PICNIC ADDITION

This pasta salad is very flavorful, attractive and easy to prepare. This is an excellent side for a bar-be-cue or buffet. Add grilled shrimp to the salad and serve it as an entrée.

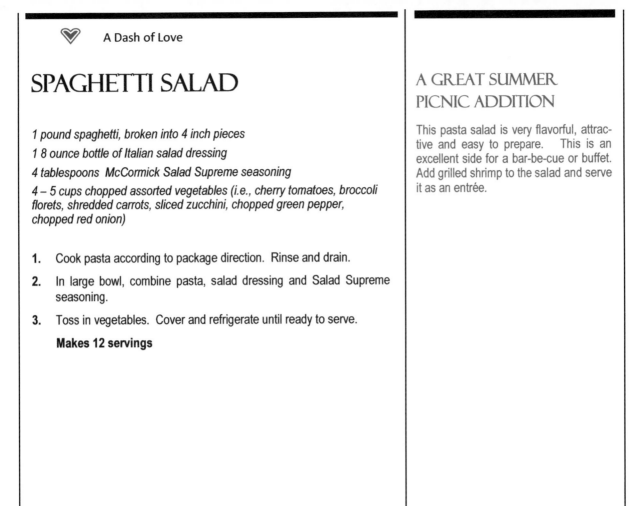

Spaghetti Salad (and Salad Supreme)

CLASSIC DELI TUNA SALAD

1 12 ounce good quality (e.g., Bumblebee) can of white albacore tuna, packed in water, drained thoroughly and flaked.

6 tablespoons real mayonnaise

2 tablespoons sour cream

1/3 cup of diced celery

2 tablespoons fresh lemon juice, preferably from Meyer lemon

Add Chef Paul Prudhomme's Magic Salmon Seasoning to taste.
(i.e., I use 1-2 teaspoons or sometimes more as it really makes a difference)

1. Thoroughly drain the tuna by opening the can, inverting the can over the drain in the sink, and then pressing on the top of the can until no more water leaks out.

2. Combine all ingredients.

3. Serve a tuna salad sandwich, an open faced tuna melt with cheddar cheese (i.e., bake at 350 degrees for 10 minutes), or plop the salad in a tomato that has been sliced and opened like a flower over a bed of lettuce.

   Serves 2 to 3

A CLASSIC DELI FAVORITE

I love tuna salad and created this recipe by experimenting over several years.

It started in college when I lived next door to a Denny's Restaurant and loved their tuna melt which was so delicious and creamy. The cook finally told me that sour cream was his secret ingredient!

Then years later I saw that the label on the Magic Salmon Seasoning suggested using this seasoning in tuna salad.

We have Meyer lemon trees now in our Rancho Santa Fe, CA "farmette" so I now add fresh lemon juice too.

Tuna Salad and Chef Paul Prudhomme's Magic Salmon Seasoning

ENTREES

"No man is lonely while eating spaghetti."

—-Robert Morley

- ♥ PORK TENDERLOIN WITH MUSTARD SAUCE

- ♥ PARMESAN CRUSTED PORK CHOPS

- ♥ STEAK AND POTATOES ON THE GRILL

- ♥ PERFECT THANKSGIVING TURKEY

- ♥ SLOW ROASTED FILET OF BEEF WITH BASIL PARMESAN MAYONNAISE

- ♥ FRAN RYAN'S LEMON CHICKEN

- ♥ CHICKEN VESUVIO

- ♥ CHICKEN WITH CRAN-CHERRY SAUCE

- ♥ CHICKEN SCHNITZEL

- ♥ COUNTRY STYLE CHICKEN KIEV

- ♥ BENGAL TIGER CHICKEN

- ♥ CHICKEN TETRAZZINI

- ♥ FAMOUS RYAN TURKEY TACOS

ENTREES CONTINUED….

- ♥ JILL'S SPECIAL CHICKEN ENCHILADAS

- ♥ CHILI VERDE

- ♥ BARBACOA

- ♥ BAKED TILAPIA

- ♥ BEER BATTERED FISH

- ♥ BARBECUED SALMON

- ♥ RAGU ALA BOLOGNAISE

- ♥ MEATBALLS WITH RICOTTA

- ♥ FETTUCCINI AL FREDO

- ♥ SAUSAGE, ROASTED PEPPERS AND SPINACH TORTA RUSTICA

- ♥ PERFECT SCRAMBLED EGGS AND BACON

- ♥ BREAKFAST   ♥

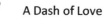

PORK TENDERLOIN WITH MUSTARD SAUCE

Pork Tenderloin

1/4 cup soy sauce

1/4 cup bourbon

2 tablespoons brown sugar

3 1-pound pork tenderloins

Mustard Sauce

1/3 cup sour cream

1/3 cup mayonnaise

1 tablespoon dry mustard

1 tablespoon finely chopped scallions

Salt to taste

1 1/2 tablespoons vinegar

1. Combine soy sauce, bourbon, and sugar. Mix well. Marinate pork in mixture 2-3 hours (or overnight) turning occasionally. Remove meat from marinade.

2. Can be grilled over hot coals or baked in a preheated 325 degree oven for 1 hour, basting occasionally.

3. Combine all sauce ingredients.   Mix well. Carve pork into 3/4 inch thick diagonal slices and serve with room-temperature sauce

Serves 5-6

A "GO-TO" ENTREE THAT YOUR GUESTS WILL LOVE

We had this pork tenderloin dish for the first time many years ago at Kathy Fanning's home. She served it with Broccoli Salad and Twice Baked Potatoes — these recipes are included in this cookbook. I can't count how many times I have made this recipe for dinner parties along with the two side dishes that Kathy made that night so many years ago.

Here's my very handsome and talented husband John Ryan who is the love of my life and a "grill master" who has made this grilled pork tenderloin many times for happy guests and hungry family members When John is not working in his real estate/construction business, he is busy, water skiing, snow skiing, surfing, playing tennis, mountain biking or paddle boarding.   John knows how to have fun and always keeps me laughing.

PARMESAN CRUSTED PORK CHOPS

4 one half inch thick pork chops

1 tablespoon olive oil

1/2 cup parmesan cheese

1/2 cup Italian bread crumbs

1 teaspoon black pepper

1 teaspoon garlic powder

1. Mix cheese and other ingredients.

Rub chops with olive oil. Coat each chop *with* crumb mixture.

1. Bake at 350 degrees for 40 minutes.

   Serves 2-3

QUICK AND DELICIOUS

It doesn't get much easier than preparing this pork chop dish on a week day evening. The   applesauce and Rice-a-Roni which I quickly learned when I married John.

Here's my wonderful father-in-law Larry Ryan, along with a picture of his prepared parmesan crusted pork chops. Larry lives most of the year in Naples, FL with his lovely wife Nancy Ryan, and in Oakbrook, IL for the rest of the year. Larry is the father of five sons and six wonderful grandchildren.   Larry is an avid tennis player who plays 3-4 times per week. Larry loves to entertain, play practical jokes, and has many friends. For many years, Larry would host the annual talent competition which we all loved. Of course our family was always the winner of the big trophy even though our talent left a lot to be desired!

STEAK AND POTATOES ON THE GRILL

T-Bone or Rib Eye Steaks
Montreal steak seasoning (found in spice aisle at grocery store)
Sweet Potatoes
Butter
Brown Sugar

1. Prepare barbecue grill with hot coals.

2. Double wrap sweet potatoes in foil and place directly onto the coals of the fire. Cook for 45 minutes to 1 hour, turning over half way through, and continue to cook until a potatoes are fork tender.

3. Lightly season steaks with Montreal Seasoning and olive oil to prevent sticking to the grill. Lightly season with Montreal steak seasoning. Grill to medium rare.

4. Unwrap potato, cut in half lengthwise and spread butter and brown sugar on each half.

A PERFECT "GOURMET" CAMPING MEAL

My nephew David Fox is an avid camper and camp cook. He loves this meal because it is so delicious and because he uses tongs to turn the steaks and potatoes and then eats them with plastic flat wear and paper plates. The only thing that must be washed is the tongs!

Here's David Fox along with a picture of his favorite steak and potatoes dish cooking on the grill. David lives in Indianapolis, IN in a beautiful home near the center of the city. David loves the outdoors, camping and fishing. David has a terrific sales management position with Groupon. David is very smart and witty and always makes me laugh.

PERFECT THANKSGIVING TURKEY

Turkey

Whole turkey, preferably fresh

2—3 Macintosh apples, peeled

Salt

8 ounces water

8 ounces turkey broth

1 cup white wine

3 ounces brandy

Turkey Rub

2 ounces olive oil

2 tablespoons butter

2 tablespoons salt

2 tablespoons paprika

2 tablespoons white pepper

1. Remove turkey from bag and remove neck and giblets. Rinse bird with cold water. Pat cavities dry lightly with paper towels Rub body and neck cavities with salt and stuff loosely.

2. Make a paste of the olive oil, butter, salt, paprika and white pepper. Rub entire turkey with the paste.

3. Place bird in open roaster breast side up. Add 8 ounces of water and 8 ounces of turkey broth to the roasting pan. Place in 325 oven.

4. When turkey is half done heat, pour white wine and brandy over turkey. Cover pan and finish baking. Let stand 30 minutes before carving.

5. These turkey drippings make a terrific starter for homemade gravy. The Mackintosh Apples that were placed in neck cavity will be soft. Mash them through a strainer and add to gravy.

THE PERFECT TURKEY IS ABSOLUTELY PERFECT

This recipe came from Lucia Pancoska, our daughter Kelly's mother-in-law. During the preparations for the wedding of Eric Pancoska and Kelly in fall of 2014 we got to know Lucia very well. She was nice enough to share her perfect turkey recipe with us so that we could make it on Thanksgiving. It truly was the best turkey (and gravy) that we ever served for Thanksgiving.

Perfect Thanksgiving Turkey

SLOW ROASTED FILET OF BEEF WITH BASIL PARMESAN MAYONNAISE

Filet of Beef

1 whole filet of beef tenderloin, trimmed and tied (4 1/2 pounds)

3 tablespoons good olive oil

4 teaspoons kosher salt

2 teaspoons coarsely ground black pepper

10 to 15 branches fresh tarragon

Basil Parmesan Mayonnaise

2 extra-large egg yolks, at room temperature

3 tablespoons freshly squeezed lemon juice

1/2 cup freshly grated Parmesan cheese

1 tablespoon Dijon mustard

1/2 cup chopped fresh basil leaves, lightly packed

1/2 teaspoon minced garlic

Kosher salt and freshly ground black pepper

1 cup vegetable oil, at room temperature

1/2 cup good olive oil, at room temperature

1. Preheat the oven to 275 degrees. Use an oven thermometer to be sure your oven temperature is accurate.

2. Place the filet on a sheet pan and pat it dry (all over) with paper towels. Brush the filet all over with the oil, reserving about half a tablespoon. Sprinkle it all over with the salt and pepper (it will seem like a lot but believe me, it makes a difference). Place the tarragon branches around the beef, tying them in 4 or 5 places with kitchen twine to keep them in place, and then brush the tarragon with the reserved oil.

3. Roast the filet of beef for 1 1/4 to 1 1/2 hours, until the temperature registers 125 degrees in the center for rare and 135 degrees for medium-rare. Cover the filet with aluminum foil and allow to rest for 20 minutes. Slice thickly and serve warm or at room temperature with Basil Parmesan Mayonnaise.

ONE OF MY PERSONAL FAVORITES

This is the perfect entrée for that special dinner or holiday party. I serve this filet of beef along with dishes that you will find in this cookbook—Broccoli Watercress Soup, Gratinee of Cauliflower and Luxembourg Salad.

Filet of Beef with Basil Parmesan Mayonnaise

FRAN RYAN'S LEMON CHICKEN

6 to 8 chicken breast halves, boneless, no skin
1/2 cup flour
1 1/2 teaspoons salt
1/4 teaspoon freshly ground pepper
1/2 teaspoon paprika, or to taste
3 tablespoons butter
2 tablespoons olive oil
1/4 cup chicken broth or water
3 tablespoons fresh lemon juice
6 to 8 thin slices of lemon
3 tablespoons capers (optional)

1. Put chicken breasts between 2 sheets of waxed paper or plastic wrap; pound to flatten with a mallet to about 1/4-inch.

2. In a shallow bowl, combine flour, salt, pepper and paprika; dredge chicken breasts to coat well.

3. Heat butter and olive oil in a large skillet. Sauté chicken breasts in batches, about 3 minutes on each side.

4. Drain off all but 2 tablespoons of fat. Stir in chicken broth, scraping to loosen browned bits. Add lemon juice and heat through. Return chicken to the skillet with the lemon slices; heat until sauce thickens. Add capers, if using. Serve with your favorite pasta and a green vegetable.

Serves 6-8

MY MOTHER-IN-LAW'S SIGNATURE DISH

When John and I were first dating he invited me to his condo in River Forest, IL for dinner. John made this lemon chicken dish for me and I was so impressed. I knew that John was good looking, smart and athletic, but I did not know that he loved to cook and did it so well!

These days John confines his culinary skills to the bar-be-que grill, but we still make this chicken dish very often with a pasta side dish and salad.

The beautiful Marriete Kaplan made this Lemon Chicken in her test kitchen in Long Grove, Illinois. Marriete is the mother of four children and a great tennis player and friend. She loves to have fun and laugh and break out into song in restaurants and bars!

CHICKEN VESUVIO

2 wings, 2 breasts, 2 legs, 2 thighs (2 or 3 pounds of chicken)

2 cloves garlic, peeled and mashed

2 teaspoons salt

1 teaspoons ground black pepper

1/3 cup olive oil

2 cups canola oil, for frying

3 large potatoes, peeled and cut into thick wedges

1 tablespoon dried oregano

1/2 cup white wine

2 tablespoons chopped parsley leaves

1. Heat oven to 400 degrees Fahrenheit.

2. Clean chicken, rinse with cold water and pat dry. Add salt and pepper. Heat 1/3-cup olive oil in a large heavy skillet over medium heat. When oil is hot, place chicken in pan .Brown well on all sides, remove chicken from pan. Pour off all but a few tablespoons of oil. Return chicken to pan and place uncovered in preheated oven for 25 minutes, turning chicken once or twice.

3. Heat 2 cups of canola oil to 350 degrees Fahrenheit. Add potato wedges into hot oil, about 4 at a time. Avoid crowding. Fry potatoes until golden and remove and let drain on paper towel and reserve for later.

4. For the last 5 minutes of cooking for the chicken, add the cooked potatoes, garlic, oregano and wine to skillet, return to oven.

5. Remove skillet from oven to stove top after the 5 minutes, add fresh parsley .

6. Arrange chicken on a large platter with potatoes atop the chicken and pour the pan juices over all.

    Serves 4

MY FAVORITE CHICKEN DISH

Chicken Vesuvio, a specialty of Chicago, is an Italian-American dish made from chicken on the bone and wedges of potato, sautéed with garlic, oregano, white wine and olive oil, then baked until the chicken's skin becomes crisp.

I love this dish and was so happy to find this recipe in the Chicago Tribune several years ago.

Chicken Vesuvio

CHICKEN WITH CRANBERRY CHERRY SAUCE

4 boneless skinless chicken breast halves
2 tablespoons unsalted butter
Flour for dredging
½ cup balsamic vinegar
1 cup cran-cherry juice
2 tablespoons honey
4 teaspoons Dijon mustard
1 cup frozen pitted dark sweet cherries

1. Pound chicken to even ½ inch thickness, season with salt and pepper.

2. Melt butter in large skillet over medium heat.

3. Dredge chicken and cook 2 minutes per side to brown lightly.

4. Remove chicken, add vinegar and scrape up browned bits from pan.

5. Whisk juice, honey and mustard into vinegar and add cherries.

6. Simmer 5 minutes until cherries begin to break apart. Transfer sauce to blender and puree.

Serves 4

SWEET AND SAVORY

This is an easy-to-prepare entrée that your family and friends will love. The cran-cherry sauce is a perfect accompaniment to the savory chicken breasts.

Here's the fabulous Barbara McClanahan along with a picture of her favorite chicken with cran-cherry sauce. I met Barbara when we first moved to California. Barbara went out of her way to include John and me in their social circle and to entertain us at her home very often. Barbara is an outstanding horse woman and tennis player and has raised two wonderful daughters to become lovely and accomplished young women. Her husband Terry is also a good friend and is my dentist too.

CHICKEN SCHNITZEL

Chicken Schnitzel

1 cup all purpose flour, seasoned with salt and white pepper

2 large eggs, lightly beaten

2 tablespoons milk

1 cup fine bread crumps

1 1/2 pounds boneless, skinless chicken breasts, pounded thin and chilled

Vegetable oil, as needed, for pan frying

Sauce

1/4 cup dry white wine

2 tablespoons fresh lemon juice

2 tablespoons heavy cream

6 tablespoons unsalted butter

2 tablespoons chopped fresh parsley

Lemon wedges, for garnish

Chicken Schnitzel

1. In a small bowl, place the seasoned flour. In a shallow container, whisk the eggs and milk together. In a medium size bowl, place the bread crumbs . Entirely coat each chicken breast with the flour, then the egg mixture, and finally the bread crumbs. Pat the chicken breasts with the bread crumbs to ensure they are completely coated. Place one layer of cutlets on a baking sheets, cover, and refrigerate at least 30 minutes before cooking.

2. Pour the oil to a 1/4 inch depth into a large skillet. Heat over medium high heat. Gently add a few cutlets at a time, and cook until golden brown on both sides, 2 to 3 minutes per side. Transfer to a baking sheet lined with absorbent paper.

3. Remove from pan and keep warm in a 200° oven until ready to serve.

Sauce

1. Deglaze pan with wine; add lemon juice and simmer 3 minutes. Add heavy cream and simmer until reduced by half, about 1 minute Off heat, whisk in butter 2 tablespoons at a time Stir in parsley; spoon sauce over medallions.

2. Serve with lemon wedges.

A TWIST ON CLASSIC GASTHOUS FOOD

I first had the traditional Austrian veal dish, Weiner Schnitzel, at the Berghoff restaurant in Chicago many years ago. I found this recipe in the Chicago Tribune a few years later and used chicken instead of veal. I prepare it and serve with mashed potatoes or if I am feeling ambitions I will make German potato salad.

Chicken Schnitzel

A Dash of Love

COUNTRY STYLE CHICKEN KIEV

2/3 cup sweet cream butter
1/2 cup fine dry bread crumbs
2 tablespoons grated Parmesan cheese
1 teaspoon each basil leaves & oregano leaves
1/2 teaspoon garlic salt
1/4 teaspoon salt
2 chicken breasts, split into 4 pieces (about 1 1/2 lb.)
1/4 cup. white wine
1/4 cup chopped green onion
1/4 cup chopped fresh parsley

1. Heat oven to 375 degrees.

2. Melt butter. Combine bread crumbs, Parmesan cheese, basil, oregano, garlic salt and salt. Dip chicken breasts in melted butter, then coat with crumb mixture; reserve remaining butter. Place chicken skin side up in ungreased baking dish.

3. Bake for 50-60 minutes or until chicken is fork tender.

4. Meanwhile, add wine, green onion and parsley to reserved melted butter (about 1/2 cup).

5. When chicken is golden brown, pour butter sauce over chicken. Continue baking for 3-5 minutes or until sauce is heated through.

6. Serve with sauce spooned over.

Serves 4

ALWAYS A HIT

My sister Barb Egofske—a fifth grade teacher—often makes this chicken dish for her family after work. It is easy to prepare, succulent and delicious enough to serve to guests too.

Here's my lovely sister Barb along with a photo of Country Style Chicken Kiev. Barb lives in Evanston Illinois with her husband Pete, and their two children, Julia and Jack. Barb likes to cycle with her club. She is a wine connoisseur wonderful hostess and fabulous sister who keeps me sane and always laughing.

BENGAL TIGER CHICKEN

8 boneless, skinless chicken breasts
1 cup real mayonnaise
1/4 teaspoon curry powder
1 1/2 cups fine Pepperidge farm dressing crumbs
1/2 cup sherry
1 can cream of chicken soup
1 tablespoon lemon juice
1 cup grated cheddar cheese
1 cup water chestnuts, sliced

1. Place chicken in buttered Pyrex dish.

2. Mix mayonnaise, curry powder, sherry, chicken soup, lemon juice and 3/4 cup of cheese. Pour over the chicken breasts.

3. Sprinkle crumbs and remaining cheese over the chicken. Dot with butter.

4. Cook for 1 1/2 hours at 350 degrees.

Serves 4 to 8

DELICIOUS AND EASY

My college friend Kathy Peterson gave me this recipe 35 years ago. I have made it for our family, as luncheon entrée for showers, and as a center-piece for a fancy dinner party.

This is named after the Bengal tiger due to the appearance of the finished dish.

Here is my college friend Kathy Peterson along with a picture of the delicious Bengal Tigers Chicken. Kathy and I were roommates back at the University of Illinois in Champagne-Urbana. Kathy is a counselor of the deaf at Hinsdale High School and is married to Rick. They have two wonderful boys. Kathy is very witty and a wonderful and generous person.

CHICKEN TETRAZZINI

WINTER COMFORT FOOD

6 large boneless chicken breasts, poached and torn into bite-sized pieces (or you can use purchased rotisserie chicken too)

½ cup butter

½ cup flour

1 teaspoon salt

½ teaspoon pepper

2 cups sliced mushrooms

2 cups chicken broth

2 cups heavy cream

4 tablespoons sherry

½ cup grated parmesan cheese

10 ounces linguine, cooked al dente

1. In a large skillet, melt butter, then add salt, pepper and flour. Stir constantly over medium heat until smooth and bubbly. Add cream and broth and stir constantly until mixture is boiling, then continue to boil for one minute. Remove from heat.

2. Stir in linguine, chicken, sherry and mushrooms. Top with parmesan cheese. Place the tetrazzini in an ungreased 2 quart casserole dish or 9 x 13 inch pan.

3. Bake uncovered until bubbly (~ 20 minutes) at 350 degrees.

Serves 6

I like to make this for dinner on a cold winter night in Chicago when the kids were growing up. My daughter Kelly loves this dish. I also substitute leftover Thanksgiving turkey for the chicken.

This is easy to make and is guaranteed to please your family and friends.

Lynn Crosby tested this Chicken Tetrazzini recipe in her Long Grove, Illinois test kitchen. Lynn has two wonderful children and is an accomplished tennis player, long-distance runner and real estate agent.

THE FAMOUS RYAN TURKEY TACOS

1 pound ground turkey (or ground beef or bison)
1/2 cup vegetable oil
3/4 cup water
1/2 chopped onion
A pinch of salt and pepper
A pinch of garlic powder
12 flat corn tortillas
1 cup shredded lettuce
1 cup diced tomatoes
2 mashed avocados
1 cup shredded cheddar cheese
1 cup sour cream
Mild or hot sauce, as needed
1 cup pico de gallo
1 diced mango

1. In a large skillet, heat vegetable oil until it starts to bubble. Place a flat tortilla in the pan. Heat each tortilla until it can be folded in half. Remove from the pan. Pat the tortilla with paper towel to remove excess oil. Continue until all 12 tortillas are done.

2. Heat another skillet to medium high heat. Add water and stir in the ground turkey, onion, salt/pepper and garlic until turkey is browned. Remove from the heat, drain and pat down the mixture to remove any excess grease.

3. Open the cooked tortilla and place the meat mixture at the bottom, then add lettuce, diced tomatoes and cheese. Serve with mashed avocados, sour cream, mango, pico de gallo and mild and hot sauces so each guest can tailor their taco to their own taste.

HAVE A TACO TUESDAY PARTY

These tacos are so good because they are made from scratch and even the tortillas are home cooked too.

Here's my fabulous sister-in-law Derilynn Ryan along with a picture of her famous Ryan tacos. Derilynn owns her own insurance business and is the mother of Doug who now works with her. Derilynn is also the loving stepmother to Conor and Bree, and stepgrandmother to Zoey. When she is not working, Derilynn is busy quilting, sewing, scrapbooking or beautifully decorating one of their homes. Derilynn and Peter split their time between Huntington Beach, CA and Livingston, Montana where they own a ranch at the foot of the mountains.

JILL'S SPECIAL CHICKEN ENCHILADAS

I medium onion chopped

2 tablespoons olive oil

1 clove garlic crushed

1 29 ounce can tomato puree

1 large can chopped green chilies

4 cups cubed or shredded cooked chicken

6 chicken bouillon cubes

I dozen medium or large flour tortillas

3 cups heavy whipping cream (or Half and Half if you must but its best with the full cream)

1 pound pepper Jack Cheese, shredded

1. Sauté onion in oil for a few minutes. Add garlic and sauté two more minutes. Add tomato puree, chilies and chicken and mix well.

2. In a separate sauce pan heat cream. Add bouillon and stir until dissolved.

3. Place chicken filling in each tortilla, roll up and arrange in greased pans. Cover with cream mixture and shredded cheese. Refrigerate overnight or up to two days.

4. Bake uncovered at 350 for 30 minutes or until bubbly. Serve with guacamole and pico del gallo and assorted salsas and top with chopped cilantro if desired.

HAVE A MEXICAN FIESTA

If you are looking for a delicious and easy Mexican dish, you have found it here. The heavy whipping cream will bring you to your knees and maybe the jack cheese will too.

Here is the fabulous Jill Stiker and a picture of her special chicken enchiladas. Jill lives in Rancho Santa Fe, CA with her husband John and triplet sons who left for different colleges this fall. I met Jill when we both served on the Rancho Santa Fe library guild. Jill is an avid runner, kayaker and overall great person and friend.

CHILE VERDE

2 tablespoons oil

3 pounds cut up pork

1 onion thinly sliced or chopped

3 chopped garlic cloves

1 teaspoon salt

1 teaspoon cumin

¾ teaspoon oregano

8-10 fresh tomatillos

1 large tomato peeled and chopped

3-4 cans Anaheim chilies chopped or 1 fresh Serrano Chile chopped finely

¼ cup fresh chopped cilantro leaves

¾ cup chicken broth

Cooked rice or fresh flour tortillas

Chopped cilantro, sour cream, Cheddar or Monterey Jack cheese and Salsa

1. Heat oil and cook pork till brown on all sides and cooked for about 10 minutes. Remove pork and add onions & garlic, sauté on medium heat till soft and then add salt, cumin and oregano.

2. In a blender add all tomatillos and puree.

3. Add tomatillos, chilies, cilantro to pan, stir in chopped tomatoes, stir in broth, then boil.

4. Add pork and simmer for 1 ½ - 2 hours.

5. Serve over rice or in a flour tortilla. Serve with chopped cilantro, sour cream, grated Cheddar or Monterey cheese and salsa.

DEEPLY FLAVORED, SUCCULENT AND COMPLEX

This fabulous Chile Verde is made by simmering rich cuts of pork in a thick stew of chilies, onions, garlic, salt, tomatillos, and little else. Braised until tender, the chili broth picks up the flavor of the melted pork fat and the uniquely sweet and bitter flavor of the chilies.

Here's Debbie Mathew with her famous Chile Verde. Debbie and I worked closely together at HP for several years—Debbie in Human Resources and me in Finance— and travelled the world on business. Debbie lives near me now in San Diego and is a good friend and fellow "Hiking Hottie" partner, an expert wine connoisseur, and a terrific cook!

BARBACOA

1/3 cup apple cider vinegar
3 tablespoons lime juice
4 chipotle peppers – canned in adobo sauce
½ sweet onion
5 cloves garlic
4 teaspoons cumin
2 teaspoons oregano
1 ½ teaspoons black pepper
1 ½ teaspoons. salt
2 teaspoons vegetable oil
4 pounds beef roast
1 cup chicken broth
3 bay leaves

1. Combine the lime juice, vinegar, onions, chipotle peppers, garlic, cumin, oregano, black pepper and salt in a blender and blend until smooth and creamy.

2. Cut the roast into smaller pieces and remove any excess fat

3. In large pot, heat 2 tsp of oil and cook meat on each side until lightly browned.

4. Transfer meat to crock pot and pour the blended sauce over the meat and add in the chicken broth and bay leaves.

5. Cook for 6+ hours, turning every hour until the meat can be easily pulled apart.

6. The broth will give the meat an extra "kick" so I recommend storing the meat in the leftover broth.

STIMULATE YOUR SENSES

Barbacoa is a form of cooking meat that originated in the Caribbean with the Taíno people, from which the term "barbecue" is derived.

Barbacoa is a simple dish that can be made into all sorts of meals. You might make tacos, burritos, extreme nachos, even hash for breakfast in the morning.

Even if you're not having thirty football crazed fans over to your house for the Super Bowl, make the full amount anyway. It's a perfect recipe to freeze for later.

Here's Terri Alonso who is a good friend and co-worker in HP Finance. Terry is a fellow "Hiking Hottie" team member and lives near me in San Diego with her husband and son. Barbacoa is Terri's signature dish and it is always a hit with her family and friends!

BAKED TILAPIA

8 Tilapia fillets
1 cup panko breadcrumbs
1 cup grated parmesan cheese
¾ cup chopped fresh parsley
½ teaspoon dried oregano
¼ teaspoon dried basil
1 teaspoon paprika
2 teaspoons salt
1 teaspoon black pepper
½ pound butter, melted
lemon wedges
parsley sprigs

1. Preheat the oven to 375°F.

2. Lightly coat a 13x9-inch baking dish with oil cooking spray or line pan with parchment paper.

3. Pat the fish dry.

4. Combine the dry ingredients in a shallow bowl and stir well.

5. Dip the tilapia in the melted butter and roll in the bread crumb mixture. Arrange the fillets in the prepared baking dish.

6. Bake uncovered for 20-30 minutes or until the fish flakes easily.

7. Garnish with lemon wedges and parsley sprigs.

ABSOLUTELY DELICIOUS !

We have tried this recipe with fresh or frozen tilapia and both work well. I make this fish often as it is so quick and easy to make and the ingredients are always available in our pantry.

If you serve this baked tilapia at an elegant dinner party, accompany the fish with a classic lemon caper butter sauce.

This is easy to make and is guaranteed to please your family and friends.

Here's our beautiful and accomplished daughter Kelly Ryan. Kelly makes this Baked Tilapia dish when she comes to visit and we love it. Kelly lives with her husband and dog Layla in San Francisco and works as a high powered salesperson for the software company Zendesk. We are so proud of Kelly and the fabulous young woman that she has become.

BEER BATTERED FISH

2 quarts vegetable oil for frying
8 fillets Walleye Pike caught in Canada (i.e., cod or other white fish can be substituted)
1 cup all purpose flour
2 tablespoons garlic powder
2 tablespoon paprika
2 teaspoons salt
2 teaspoons ground black pepper
1 egg, beaten
12 ounces beer

1. Heat oil in deep fryer to 365 degrees F. Rinse fish, pat dry, and season with salt and pepper.

2. Combine flour, garlic powder, paprika, 2 teaspoons salt and 2 teaspoons pepper. Stir egg into dry ingredients. Gradually mix in beer until a thin batter is formed. You should be able to see the fish through the batter after it has been dipped.

3. Dip fish fillets into the batter, then drop one at a time into hot oil. Fry fish, turning once, until both sides are golden brown. Drain on paper towels, and serve warm.

Serves 8

FROM LAKE TO TABLE

Every June for the past 20+ years my brother--in-law Pete Egofske and his "fishin" buddies drive 14 hours to Canada to spend the week fishing for Walleye Pike. Pete and my sister Barb (his wife) host a big fish fry each summer with 50 of their closest friends to consume the fish caught in Canada. It is always fun and the fish is fabulous.

Here's Dr. Peter Egofske, my brother-in-law, along with a picture of his Beer Battered Walleye Pike that he caught in Canada. Pete is an Interventional Radiologist at Stroger Hospital in Chicago. Pete and Barb live in Evanston, Illinois with their two children. Pete is a marathon runner, big-time fly fisherman and loves to blow leaves or anything from his lawn, sidewalk or patio. I've known Pete since he was in high school and introduced him to my sister Barb who he later married.

BARBECUED SALMON

1 tablespoon butter
1 tablespoon honey
1 tablespoon firmly packed brown sugar
2 tablespoons soy sauce
3 tablespoons Dijon mustard
1 tablespoon olive oil
1 teaspoon minced fresh ginger or garlic
1 salmon filet with skin (3 1/2 to 4 1/2 pounds)
Lime slices and wedges
Whole cloves (optional)

1. In a 6-8 inch frying pan over medium hear, stir butter with honey and brown sugar until butter melts. Remove from heat; add to pan the soy, mustard, oil and ginger; mix well. Let sauce cool slightly.

2. Meanwhile, rinse fish and pat dry. To make fish easier to handle when cooked, set it skin down on a large piece of foil, rip foil (or fold under) to fit outline of fish. Set fish and foil in a rimmed pan large enough to hold the fish. Stir sauce and spoon evenly over fish; let stand 15 minutes to 1 hour; frequently spoon sauce over fish.

3. Put salmon with foil on a grill over indirect heat. Cover barbecue grill with lid, open any vents, and cook until fish is opaque, but still moist-looking in thickest part (i.e., cut to test), 20-30 minutes. To move fish onto a platter, support with 2 large spatulas, or slip a rimless baking sheet under fish. Set, or slide fish onto a platter.

4. Serve salmon hot or cold; if making ahead, cover and chill up to 1 day. Squeeze juice from lime wedges onto portions.

Serves 10 to 12

DELECTABLE !

A simple soy sauce and brown sugar marinade, with hint of ginger and mustard, are the perfect salty-sweet complement to rich salmon filets. This is an elegant addition to holiday parties, buffet dinners, and family get-togethers.

Here's my friend Dana Gross, who lives near us in San Diego and we hike together in our "Hiking Hotties" group. Dana is a "foodie" who lived for awhile in the Pacific northwest where she acquired this fabulous salmon recipe. Dana is married to Jeff and has two beautiful daughters.

RAGU ALA BOLOGNESE

1 28 ounce can whole peeled tomatoes (with juice)
1/4 cup extra-virgin olive oil
1 rib celery, finely chopped
1/2 medium yellow onion, finely chopped
1/2 medium carrot, finely chopped
Kosher salt and freshly ground black pepper, to taste
1 1/4 pound ground beef chuck
1/2 pound pork shoulder
1 4 ounce piece of pancetta, finely chopped
2 cups dry red wine
2 tablespoons tomato paste

1. Puree the tomatoes and their juice in a blender until smooth

2. Heat the oil and butter in a large heavy-bottomed pan over medium heat. Add the celery, onion and carrots, season with salt and pepper, and cook, stirring frequently, until soft and lightly browned, about 15 minutes. Reduce heat to low and cook, stirring occasionally, until very soft and caramelized, about 15 minutes more.

3. Add the beef and pork and cook, stirring and breaking up meat with a wooden spoon, until the meat begins to brown, about 10 minutes. Add the pancetta and continue cooking, stirring occasionally, until its fat has rendered, about 10 minutes more. Increase the heat to medium, add the wine, and simmer, stirring constantly, until evaporated, about 5 minutes. Add tomato paste and cook stirring frequently, for 2 minutes.

4. Add reserved tomato puree, reduce to low and simmer, stirring occasionally until sauce is very thick, about 3 hours. (You can also cook the ragu in the oven at 275 degrees for 3 hours if you would prefer not to cook this on the stove.)

5. Season ragu with salt and pepper. Toss with fresh tagliatelle or the pasta of your choice or use in lasagna. Serve with grated parmesan cheese.

AN AUTHENTIC ITALIAN DISH

Pasta Bolognese is my favorite dish to order when at an Italian restaurant. I had often tried to prepare Bolognese sauce myself, but could never quite duplicate that fabulous, rich, meaty flavor until I discovered this recipe when attending a cooking class at Sur La Table. I have made it a few times since then and it is so delicious!

Ragu ala Bolognese over Pasta

MEATBALLS WITH RICOTTA

2 pounds ground beef
1 pound Ricotta cheese
4 large eggs, whisked until combined
8 ounces shredded white bread
1/4 teaspoons pepper
1 1/2 teaspoons salt
1/4 cup grated parmesan or romano cheese
Olive oil

1. In a large bowl mix all ingredients with your hands only until combined. Do not over mix or the meatballs will be less tender and too dense.

2. Form into meatballs. Heat 1/2 inch of olive oil in bottom of large pot. Cook the meatballs in batches until cooked through turning so as to brown all sides.

3. Add meatballs to your favorite marinara sauce and serve with pasta or on sandwiches.

ABBONDANZA!!

These meatballs are the lightest, most tender and delicious that I have ever tasted. This Capasso family recipe came from Joanne Capasso Balogh, who gave it to me after I had the pleasure of being served these marvelous meatballs for the first time.

Here's the lovely Joanne Balogh along with a picture of her fabulous meatballs. Even though we live 2,000 miles apart these days we still talk often and get together to shop, eat and conduct "wine tasting." Joanne volunteers at the Lake country district attorneys office, and likes to golf, play tennis and of course shop, shop and shop.

FETTUCCINI AL FREDO

1/2 pound butter
1 3 ounce package of cream cheese
1 pint half and half
1 cup milk
3 cloves garlic, crushed
3 ounces parmesan cheese
1 pound fettuccine

1. Melt butter in a large sauce pan. Add crushed garlic and simmer for 7 to 10 minutes, being careful not to allow butter to brown.

2. Add cream cheese, half & half and milk. Heat slowly for 10 minutes. Discard garlic.

3. Add cooked fettuccine noodles to the al fredo sauce and simmer over very low heat for 5 minutes or until the sauce can absorb enough starch from the pasta to reach the appropriate consistency. Remove from heat and toss with parmesan cheese.

Serves 4.

LOVE AT FIRST SIGHT

This fettuccine al fredo recipe is an adaption of the original pasta dish made with parmesan cheese and butter. To add creaminess and even more richness, cream cheese and milk are also added. As the cream and parmesan cheeses melt, it emulsifies with the milk to form a smooth and rich coating on the pasta.

This recipe originated from John's mother (i.e., my mother-in-law), Fran Ryan. John made this for me when we were dating and I fell in love with the pasta and HIM!

Here is my dear mother-in-law, who died several years ago, and whom we miss so much. She was a great mother to her five devoted boys, champion tennis player and terrific cook. Also pictured is Fran's famous Fettuccine Alfredo. Fran is loved by all who knew her .

SAUSAGE, ROASTED PEPPER AND SPINACH TORTA RUSTICA

16 - 1/4-inch-thick baguette slices, cut on slight diagonal
1 tablespoon butter
12 ounces fresh baby spinach leaves
1 pound sweet Italian sausage, casing removed
1 1/2 cups grated Fontina cheese, divided
3/4 cup diced drained roasted red peppers (from 12-ounce jar)
6 large eggs
1 cup heavy whipping cream
1 cup whole milk
1 teaspoon coarse kosher salt
1/4 teaspoon ground black pepper

1. Preheat oven to 350°F. Butter 8x8x2-inch baking dish.

2. Place 8 baguette slices in bottom of dish; press 2 baguette slices onto each side.

3. Melt 1 tablespoon butter in large pot over medium-high heat. Add spinach; toss until just wilted, about 3 minutes. Transfer spinach to strainer; cool. Squeeze spinach dry. Transfer to medium bowl.

4. Heat same pot over medium-high heat. Add sausage. Sauté until cooked through, breaking up, about 7 minutes. Mix into spinach; mix in 1 cup cheese and peppers. Spread atop baguette slices in bottom of dish. Whisk eggs in medium bowl to blend.

5. Whisk in last 4 ingredients. Pour over spinach mixture and stir lightly with fork to distribute evenly. Sprinkle remaining 1/2 cup cheese over.

6. Bake torta until puffed and golden and center is set, about 55 minutes. Remove from oven and let rest 15 minutes before serving.

Serves 8.

A BRUNCH CENTERPIECE

This is not your typical egg casserole. The spinach, Italian sausage and Fontina cheese, together with the eggs, bring together flavors that create a creamy, substantial and succulent dish.

My friend Suzanne Johnson made this Torta Rustica for us and then passed on the recipe. Since then I have made this on Easter morning to rave reviews.

Here is the lovely Vicki Petersen holding the Torta Rustica at Joan Delott's Oscar Party. The Torta was made in Vicki's Lincolnshire, IL "test kitchen." Vicki has three fabulous grown children. Vicki is an A-rated tennis player, successful real estate agent, and owner of "Vicki's Gifts" where she sells ladies accessories. Everyone loves Vicki for her fabulous sense of humor and inclusive personality.

PERFECT SCRAMBLED EGGS AND BACON

Julia Child's Perfect Scrambled Eggs
2 eggs
1 pad of butter
1 tablespoons (or thereabouts) of whole milk or cream
Salt and pepper to taste

Perfect Bacon
1 package good quality bacon
Parchment paper

Perfect Scrambled Eggs

1. Heat a medium pan (preferably nonstick) over medium-low heat.

2. In a separate bowl, scramble your eggs enough to break the yolks and mix the whites in, but not enough to make the mixture frothy. In other words, don't over mix.

3. When the pan is heated, reduce the heat to low and add the butter. Once the butter melts along the bottom of the pan, add your eggs and let them sit for a bit in the butter. Don't stir too quickly. You want the heat to permeate the bottom of the eggs and start to cook them.

4. When you can see that the bottom of the eggs have begun to heat through, stir the eggs and then add the cream or milk, which will instantly froth a bit. Mix the milk or cream into so it integrates into the eggs and makes them custardy.

5. Continue cooking on low heat until the eggs are slightly firm (but not so long that they are actually firm).

6. Remove from the pan and serve immediately with salt and pepper to taste.

Perfect Bacon

1. Line a cookie sheet with parchment paper, leaving several inches of paper on all sides of the pan to allow for easy clean up.

2. Place bacon slices side by side on the cookie sheet.

3. Bake in 375 degree preheated oven (convention setting) for 15 to 18 minutes or until bacon reaches desired level of crispness.

4. Remove bacon from oven and drain on paper towels.

5. Gather up parchment paper to capture all of the bacon grease and toss into trash.

6. Place unused cooked bacon in plastic freezer bag side by side and freeze. Frozen bacon can be reheated for 15 seconds in the microwave.

PARIS INSPIRED

When in Paris I found that the scrambled eggs served in our hotel were so beautifully creamy and light. When I returned I found this recipe from Julia Child which enabled me to duplicate those wonderful Parisian eggs.

You can vary this recipe a bit by adding some cheese or chives toward the end (just after you add the milk) or starting out with some bacon or ham in the pan. Better yet, cook some onions in the butter first and then scramble the eggs. Or top with some caviar if you want a luxurious meal.

The world is really your oyster when it comes to scrambled eggs. Eat them plain or with your favorite topping, just be sure to cook them with care.

Perfect Scrambled Eggs and Bacon

BREAKFAST

Coffee, sugar and cream
1 package sausage links-maple flavored
1 green pepper, chopped
1 red pepper, chopped
1 deli package of mushrooms, washed
1/4 - 1/2 package of shredded cheese- your choice.
8-10 eggs
Spray oil.
Salt
Pepper.

.

1. Make coffee.
2. Heat up an electric griddle or fry pan.
3. Make sausage links. Cook until done. Place on a plate and cover to keep warm.
4. While cooking sausage chop up 1-2 green peppers, onions, fresh mushrooms.
5. Crack the eggs in a bowl and beat the eggs to mix with a fork. Set to the side.
6. Remove any grease and lightly spray oil the surface of the pan. Add peppers, onions and mushrooms to the surface and cook on low until soften and hot.
7. Slowly add eggs to the vegetable mixture and add cheese, salt and pepper.
8. Gently mix eggs with a spatula to thoroughly cook.
9. Pour coffee in cups.
10. Bring all food to the table and eat.

Serves 4—5

THE MOST IMPORTANT MEAL OF THE DAY

Randy Fox, my brother-in-law, loves to make breakfast and never deviates from the process as shown here. It is guaranteed to produce the "perfect" breakfast according to Randy.

Here's a picture of Randy Fox along with his favorite breakfast items. Randy lives in Pittsboro, IN with my sister Susan (his wife) and is a college teacher, and is an avid fisherman and camper. Randy is building a beautiful log cabin on their property in southern Indiana, which Susan is excited for him to finish. Randy is the father of two wonderful children and the grandfather of two.

SIDE DISHES

"No Life expectancy would grow by leaps and bounds if green vegetables smelled as good as bacon."

—— Doug Larson

- MUSHROOM FARRO RISOTTO

- GREEN BEANS WITH GARLIC AND LEMON

- TWICE BAKED POTATOES

- CALICO BAKED BEANS

- LOBSTER MACARONI AND CHEESE

- MACARONI AND CHEESE

- THANKSGIVING STUFFING

- PERFECT CRANBERRY SAUCE

- BRAISED KALE WITH BACON

- SPINACH AND CHEESE CASSEROLE

- SWEET POTATO PRALINE

- GRATINEE OF CAULIFLOWER

- HOLIDAY HAM STUFFING

- CORN PUDDING

MUSHROOM FARRO RISOTTO

1/2 ounce dried porcini mushrooms
1 quart vegetable broth
1 1/2 cups cracked farro (can be found near the rice in the grocery store)
2 tablespoons extra virgin olive oil
1/2 cup onions, finely chopped
1 pound cremini mushrooms or 1 pound wild mushrooms, cleaned, trimmed and sliced
Salt
2 garlic cloves, minced
2 teaspoons fresh rosemary, chopped
1/2 cup dry white wine
1/3 cup parmesan cheese, grated
1/4 cup fresh parsley, chopped

1. Place the farro in a bowl, and pour on enough hot water to cover by an inch. Let soak according to package instructions (i.e., some types of farro must be soaked overnight).

2. Place the dried mushrooms in a large bowl. Cover with 2 cups boiling water. Let sit 30 minutes.

3. Drain the mushrooms through a strainer set over a bowl and lined with a paper towel. Squeeze the mushrooms over the strainer, then rinse in several changes of water to remove grit. Chop coarsely. Set aside.

4. Add the broth from the mushrooms to the stock. You should have 6 cups (add water if necessary). Place in a saucepan, and bring to a simmer. Salt to taste.

5. Heat oil over medium heat in a large skillet. Add the onion. Cook, stirring, until it begins to soften, about three minutes.

6. Add the fresh mushrooms. Cook, stirring, until they begin to soften and sweat. Add salt to taste, garlic and rosemary. Continue to cook, stirring often, until the mushrooms are tender, about five minutes.

7. Add the farro and dried mushrooms. Cook, stirring, until the grains of farro are separate and beginning to crackle, about two minutes.

8. Stir in the wine and cook, stirring until the wine has been absorbed.

9. Add all but about 1 cup of the stock, and bring to a simmer. Cover and simmer until the farro is tender, about 50 minutes. Remove the lid, and stir vigorously from time to time. Taste and adjust seasoning.

10. There should be some liquid remaining in the pot but not too much. If the farro is submerged in stock, raise the heat and cook until there is just enough to moisten the grains, like a sauce. If there is not, stir in the remaining stock. Add the Parmesan, parsley and fresh ground pepper to taste, and stir together. Remove from the heat and serve.

Serves 6—8

FOR MUSHROOM LOVERS

This is a fabulous side dish with beef or can be served as a stand alone entrée with a salad for a casual dinner. I had this the first time when dining at my friend Marie Campagna's home. Marie gave me the recipe and I have made this numerous times to rave reviews. It takes some time to prepare but it is worth it. This is both delicious and healthy!!

Here is the lovely Marie Campagna along with a picture of the Mushroom Farro Risotto. Marie and her husband Mike split their time between Rancho Santa Fe, CA and LaGrange, IL. Marie was formerly a managing partner with the consulting firm, Accenture. She is retired now but stays very busy by managing her avocado farm, fruit orchard, vegetable garden and vast rose garden. I am the lucky recipient of the bounty from her garden. Marie has it all ... she is smart, pretty, interesting and amazingly generous.

GREEN BEANS WITH GARLIC AND LEMON

2 pounds green beans, ends trimmed
1 tablespoon extra-virgin olive oil
3 tablespoons butter
2 large garlic cloves, minced
1 teaspoon red pepper flakes
1 tablespoon lemon zest
Salt and freshly ground black pepper

1. Blanch green beans in a large stock pot of well salted boiling water until bright green in color and tender crisp, roughly 2 minutes. Drain and shock in a bowl of ice water to stop from cooking.

2. Heat a large heavy skillet over medium heat. Add the oil and the butter. Add the garlic and red pepper flakes and sauté until fragrant, about 30 seconds. Add the beans and continue to sauté until coated in the butter and heated through, about 5 minutes. Add lemon zest and season with salt and pepper.

Serves 8

SIMPLE AND ELEGANT

This recipe for green beans came from my niece Sarah Farrell, who made this as a side dish for Thanksgiving dinner. These green beans are the perfect accompaniment to any entrée. The cooking technique of shocking the green beans in cold water guarantees that the green beans stay bright green and tender crisp.

Here is Carrie McConachie, a beautiful and very accomplished friend, along with the green beans with garlic and lemon which she prepared in her test kitchen in Long Grove, Illinois and which she brought to Joan Delott's Oscar party to share with the gang. Carrie has two sons and works as an IT executive for McDonald's Corporation.

TWICE BAKED POTATOES

8 baking potatoes, washed
3 tablespoons canola oil
2 sticks salted butter
1 cup bacon bits (fry your own!)
1 cup sour cream
1 cup Cheddar or Jack cheese (or a mix of both), plus more for topping
1/2 cup heavy cream
2 teaspoons seasoned salt
3 green onions, sliced
Freshly ground black pepper

1. Preheat the over to 400 degrees. Place the potatoes on a baking sheet. Rub them with the canola oil and bake for 1 hour, making sure they're sufficiently cooked through.

2. Slice the butter into pats. Place in a large mixing bowl and add the bacon bits and sour cream. Remove the potatoes from the oven. Lower the heat to 350 degrees F.

3. With a sharp knife, cut each potato in half lengthwise. Scrape out the insides into the mixing bowl, being careful not to tear the shell. Leave a small rim of potato intact for support. Lay the hollowed out potato shells on a baking sheet.

4. Smash the potatoes into the butter, bacon and sour cream. Add the cheese, milk, seasoned salt, green onions and black pepper to taste and mix together well. Do not use an electric mixer as it will make the potatoes "gluey." (IMPORTANT: If you plan to freeze the twice-baked potatoes, do NOT add the green onions.)

5. Fill the potato shells with the filling. I like to fill the shells so they look abundant and heaping. Top each potato with a little more grated cheese and pop 'em in the oven until the potato is warmed through, 15 to 20 minutes.

Serves 12

QUITE YUMMY

When I serves these potatoes my guests often say, "These are the best potatoes I have ever eaten!" It is not my cooking technique that makes the difference. The secret to these twice baked potatoes is the liberal use of butter, sour cream, heavy cream and cheese. I don't tell anyone my secret so as not to horrify our calorie and fat conscious guests—it is ok for them to splurge every now and then, especially at my house!

Cheesy Baked Potatoes

CALICO BAKED BEANS

1 lb. sliced bacon, cooked and broken into 1 inch bits
1 1/2 pounds ground beef, cooked and crumbled
1 pound 12 ounce can of pork and beans
2 - 15 ounce cans of white navy beans
1 cup packed brown sugar
1 cup of your favorite bar-be-sauce
1 envelope dry onion soup mix

1. Mix ingredients in large baking dish.

2. Bake at 350 degrees Fahrenheit for one hour.

   Serves a Crowd

GOURMET BAKED BEANS

I am normally not a baked beans fan, but these baked beans are exceptional. They are so tasty and are the absolute right consistency — not too thick and not too watery. And they contain our favorite food: BACON!

Kathy Fanning served this dish to us many, many years ago. I took her recipe and it has been a staple for my guests ever since.

Here is Kathy Fanning, the "hostess with the mostest," along with her famous baked beans. Notice that the picture of the baked beans are flanked by croquet balls as Kathy ALWAYS serves this at her outdoor barbeque parties (and indoor buffets too.) Kathy lives in Inverness, Illinois with her husband Kevin, has 3 accomplished children and is the CFO of Smith Gill architecture firm. Kathy is the salt of the earth.

LOBSTER MACARONI AND CHEESE

4 tablespoons butter, plus 1 tablespoon for greasing dish

Kosher salt

1 pound penne pasta

2 small shallots, finely chopped

2 cloves garlic, chopped

Freshly ground black pepper

2 tablespoons tomato paste

5 tablespoons all-purpose flour

1/4 cup white wine

4 cups heavy cream

1/2 teaspoon sweet paprika

1/4 teaspoon cayenne pepper

1 bay leaf

2 cups shredded sharp white Cheddar

2 cups shredded Gruyere

2 (8-ounce) raw lobster tails, defrosted if frozen, meat removed from shell, chopped

1/4 cup panko bread crumbs

1/4 cup freshly chopped parsley leaves

1. Preheat the oven to 350 degrees F and adjust racks to the middle. Grease a 13 by 9-inch baking dish with butter.

2. In a large pot of boiling salted water over medium heat, add the pasta and cook until al dente. Drain the pasta and reserve.

3. Add 4 tablespoons butter to a large pot over medium heat. Once the butter shimmers, add the shallots and garlic and sauté until translucent. Season with salt and pepper, to taste. Add the tomato paste and flour and stir to toast, about 3 to 4 minutes. Add the white wine and reduce by half, about 2 minutes. Slowly add the cream, whisking well to remove any lumps. Add the paprika, cayenne, and bay leaf. Bring the cream up to a simmer and turn the heat to low. Let reduce until the cream is thick and can coat a spoon, about 5 to 10 minutes. When thickened, remove the bay leaves.

4. Stir in the grated cheeses, a handful at a time, combining well after each addition. Add the chopped lobster meat to the sauce and stir well. Add the pasta and stir. Add to the greased baking dish and sprinkle with the panko crumbs and parsley. Bake for 25 minutes. Remove from the oven and let rest for 10 minutes before serving. Sprinkle individual servings with parsley.

THANKSGIVING SIDE DISH?

My niece, Sarah Farrell, makes lobster macaroni and cheese as a side dish for Thanksgiving dinner. It is so delectable that it upstages the stuffing, potatoes and all of the other Thanksgiving goodies. But boy do we love it!

Lobster Macaroni and Cheese, with it's cheesy goodness and rich lobster sweetness, can also be served as the main dish at even a fancy dinner party. It's that good.

My niece Sarah Farrell loves to cook in her spare time, when not working at her demanding investment banking position in Manhattan or perfecting her ballet technique. Sarah attacks everything she does with drive and perfection which is why every dish she creates — cakes, roasted vegetables or Lobster Mac and Cheese — are always fabulous.

MACARONI AND CHEESE

1 cup finely diced onion

5 tablespoons butter

4 tablespoons flour

4 cups whole milk

36 ounces grated cheddar cheese

1 pound of cavatappi pasta

Salt and pepper to taste

1. In a large saucepan, cook onion in butter until soft, but not browned, about 6 minutes.

2. Stir in flour to make a roux.

3. Whisk in milk and put on medium heat and stir until it just begins to thicken.

4. Remove from heat and fold in 24 ounces shredded cheddar cheese.

5. Add salt and pepper to cheese mixture. Cheese should be melted from the remnant heat.

6. At the same time as above, cook one pound of Cavatappi pasta until al dente. Drain, don't rinse. Pour into the prepared cheese sauce and mix.

7. Pour the mixture into a large buttered baking dish.

8. Cook for about 20 minutes in preheated 400-degree oven. Take out of the oven and add 12 ounces of grated cheddar cheese on top. Cook in the oven for another 15 minutes until it is hot throughout and bubbling. Don't cook too long or cheese gets tough and oily! You can also add Parmesan cheese on top instead of some of the cheddar, and breadcrumbs sautéed in butter.

GLORIOUS AND CHEESY

This recipe for traditional macaroni and cheese comes from the Thyme in the Ranch restaurant in Rancho Santa Fe., a wonderful spot for lunch or coffee and pastries.

Macaroni and cheese is the quintessential comfort food that is loved by all.

Here is the beautiful Sophia Alsadek along with a picture of her macaroni and cheese. Sophia lives in Rancho Santa Fe where she has countless friends, a terrific husband, Louay, and two wonderful boys. Sophia is an avid college football fan and philanthropist. Sophia's engaging, confident and inclusive personality draws other people to her. Sophia always makes me laugh!

THANKSGIVING STUFFING

8 cups (1/2-inch) pieces firm white bread (3/4 pounds)

1 1/2 pounds fresh pork sausage meat, crumbled

1/2 stick (1/4 cup) unsalted butter

2 onions, chopped

3 celery ribs, sliced 1/4inch thick

1 Granny Smith apple, peeled and cut into 1/2-inch pieces

2 teaspoons minced garlic

1 1/2 cups chopped pecans (8 ounces), toasted

1 cup dried cranberries

1 tablespoon chopped fresh sage

1. Preheat oven to 350°F.

2. Toast bread in a large shallow baking pan in middle of oven until dry and pale golden, about 20 minutes.

3. Cook sausage in a large heavy skillet over moderately high heat, stirring and breaking up large lumps, until no longer pink, about 5 minutes, then transfer with a slotted spoon to a large bowl.

4. Add butter to fat remaining in skillet and cook onions, stirring, until softened, about 7 minutes. Add celery, apple, and garlic and cook, stirring, 2 minutes. Transfer to bowl with sausage and stir in bread, pecans, cranberries, sage, and salt and pepper to taste.

5. Transfer stuffing to a buttered 3- to 4-quart shallow baking dish and drizzle with broth. (Use 1 1/2 cups broth if you like a moist stuffing, 1 cup if you prefer it drier.) Cover with foil and bake in middle of oven 30 minutes, then uncover and bake until bread is golden and stuffing is heated through, 20 to 25 minutes more.

6. Cooks' note: Stuffing can be assembled (but not baked), without nuts, 1 day ahead and chilled, covered. Toss in pecans and bring to room temperature before baking.

INSPIRED BY GRAM'S OLD FASHIONED STUFFING

My Grandmother Burke used to make stuffing from toasted bread on Thanksgiving morning and always added pork sausage, onions and celery. I have since added apples, cranberries and pecans to jazz it up.

Here's my friend Nanette Kelley, displaying the Thanksgiving Stuffing that she made in her Jupiter, Florida "test kitchen." Nanette and I met when we both played tennis at Royal Melbourne in Long Grove and became fast friends. We played bridge, "lunched," and had a blast! I love visiting Nanette in her ocean front condo in Florida and swimming together in the Atlantic ocean. Nanette is married to Russ and has two wonderful grown daughters.

PERFECT CRANBERRY SAUCE

1 12-ounce bag of fresh cranberries

1 cup sugar

1 strip orange or lemon zest

1 cup of water

1. Empty cranberries into a saucepan and transfer 1/2 cup to a small bowl. Add 1 cup sugar, orange or lemon zest and water to the pan and cook over low heat, stirring occasionally, until the sugar dissolves and the cranberries are soft, about 10 minutes. Increase the heat to medium and cook until the cranberries burst, about 12 minutes.

2. Reduce the heat to low and stir in the reserved cranberries. Add sugar, salt and pepper to taste and cool to room temperature before serving

Serves 8 to 10

THANKSGIVING STAPLE

My brother Jim Martin always brings the cranberries for Thanksgiving dinner. When we moved to San Diego, I had to learn to make them myself!

I use these cranberries with the leftover turkey and stuffing to make sandwiches on the day after Thanksgiving. Fabulous!

Here's my brother Jim Martin along with the Perfect Cranberries. Jim lives in Vernon Hills, Illinois and loves to exercise (he does it daily — rain or shine) and to bird watch. Jim is the foremost authority on most subjects and is a fascinating conversationalist on anything from British Royal history to the NASA space program to the Vietnam War to any current event. I ask Jim when I need clarification on what is really happening in the world!!!

BRAISED KALE WITH BACON

4 thick slices of bacon

2 tablespoons extra-virgin olive oil

1 large onion, thinly sliced

2 garlic cloves, minced

1 1/2 pounds kale, stems and inner ribs discarded, leaves coarsely chopped, washed and dried

Salt and freshly ground pepper

1 1/2 tablespoons white wine vinegar

1. In a large, deep skillet, cook the bacon in the oil over moderately high heat, turning once, until crisp, about 6 minutes. Drain the bacon on paper towels, leaving the fat in the skillet. Coarsely chop the bacon.

2. Add the onion and garlic to the skillet and cook over moderate heat, stirring occasionally, until softened and lightly browned, about 6 minutes. Add the kale, season with salt and pepper and toss until slightly wilted. Stir in the vinegar, cover and cook over high heat until the kale is tender, about 5 minutes. Stir in the chopped bacon and serve.

Serves 4 to 6

NUTRITIOUS AND DELICIOUS

I have tried Kale in several ways—cold in salads, steamed, etc.—given its health benefits, but until I found this recipe I simply didn't like its bitterness. The addition of the bacon and garlic, plus sautéing for a few minutes makes it very delicious.

Here is my good friend Joan Delott displaying the Braised Kale that she made in her Long Grove, Illinois "test kitchen" and served at her Oscar Party. While Joan does not enjoy cooking all that much, when she does undertake a recipe it is always magnificent! Joan is a great tennis player and has a business in which she sells clothing and her signature handmade bracelets and necklaces.

FRAN RYAN'S SPINACH AND CHEESE CASSEROLE

20 ounces frozen chopped spinach, (thawed)

1 onion (chopped)

2 garlic cloves (minced)

8 tablespoons butter (melted)

6 eggs (beaten)

16 ounces low fat cottage cheese (2 cups)

2 tablespoons all-purpose flour

1 pound low-fat sharp cheddar cheese (grated approx. 4 cups)

Salt

1. Preheat oven to 350 degrees. Lightly grease a 13 x 9 inch baking dish.

2. Drain spinach well by squeezing out all of the liquid.. Saute onion and garlic in 2 tablespoons of the melted butter.

3. Mix spinach with eggs, cottage cheese and cheddar cheese. Add sautéed onions and garlic. Season with salt and pepper.

4. Pour into prepared dish and bake for 1 hour.

Serves 4 to 6

ENTRÉE, SIDE DISH OR APPETIZER

This is a signature dish of my mother-in-law Fran Ryan and one of three recipes that my husband John made for me before we were married. Fran always was careful to make healthy yet delicious food and this Spinach and Cheese Casserole recipe is exactly that.

Here is Joy Kruyswyk displaying the Spinach and Cheese Casserole that she made in her Long Grove, IL "test kitchen" and served at Joan Delott's Oscar Party. Joy is a successful employment attorney in Chicago and has three terrific boys who love their mom. Joy and Matt also have a home in Florida where they get away from those cold Chicago winters to bask in the sun.

SWEET POTATO PRALINE

Sweet Potatoes

3 cups mashed sweet potatoes

1 cup sugar

½ cup melted butter

1 tsp. vanilla

½ cup fresh orange juice

2 eggs, beaten

Topping

½ cup brown sugar

¼ cup flour

2-1/2 tablespoons melted butter

½ cup pecans, chopped

1. Mix all sweet potato ingredients together and pour into a 2 quart casserole dish.

2. Top with crumbled topping. Bake at 350 degrees for 25 minutes.

   Serves 4 to 6

IT DOESN'T HAVE TO BE THANKSGIVING

These sweet potatoes are so good that you will want to serve this as a side dish throughout the year, not just Thanksgiving.

Here is the beautiful Kristine Clarke displaying the Sweet Potato Praline recipe that she prepared in her Hawthorn Woods, IL "test kitchen" and served at Joan Delott's Oscar Party. Kristine is an avid tennis player and wonderful Mom, who has many devoted friends who love Kristine for her sweet disposition and fun loving attitude.

GRATINEE OF CAULIFLOWER

6 tablespoons unsalted butter

4 cloves garlic, minced

4 ounces thinly sliced prosciutto, cut into thin strips

Florets of 1 large head cauliflower, cut into ¼ inch lengthwise slides

2 tablespoons unbleached all-purpose flour

1-1/2 cups heavy or whipping cream

Pinch cayenne pepper

Salt and freshly ground black pepper, to taste

1-1/2 cups grated gruyere or Swiss cheese

1. Preheat oven to 350 degrees.

2. Melt butter in a large skillet over medium heat. Add the garlic and saute 2 minutes. Stir in the prosciutto and sauté 2 minutes more.

3. Add the cauliflower and cook just until it begins to lose its crispness, 3 or 4 minutes.

4. Stir in the flour and then the cream. Blend well. Season with the cayenne and salt and pepper to taste. Heat to boiling and immediately remove from heat.

5. Pour the cauliflower into a shallow au gratin dish. Top with the cheese and parsley. Bake until the top is lightly browned and bubbling, about 30 minutes. Serve immediately.

Serves 6

UNFORGETTABLE

When growing up I had never been a cauliflower fan probably because I had only tasted steamed cauliflower. I love cauliflower now that I found this delicious gratinee recipe. The gruyere cheese, prosciutto, garlic, butter and cream together create a perfect backdrop for the now beloved cauliflower.

I serve this for special holiday and dinner parties as an accompaniment to beef or ham.

Here is the lovely and accomplished Gail Nelson with the Gratinee of Cauliflower that she made in her Long Grove, IL "test kitchen." Gail literally saved my life by stepping in several years ago to help me navigate my breast cancer treatment process. Gail is a sales executive who balances her demanding job, her family of two wonderful daughters and husband Rich, and her wide network of devoted friends. Gail is one of those people who always make whomever she is speaking to feel special and loved.

HOLIDAY HAM STUFFING

1/2 cup salted butter or 1/2 cup margarine, softened

1/2-3/4 cup sugar (or adjust to taste)

1 pinch salt (less than 1/8 teaspoon and add in only if using unsalted butter or margarine)

4 eggs

1 (20 ounce) cans crushed pineapple, drained

5 slices day old bread, cubed

1. Set oven to 350 degrees F. Grease a 9-inch baking pan.

2. In a medium bowl cream the butter or margarine with sugar and salt (if using) until fluffy. Add in eggs and beat until well combined. Mix the drained crushed pineapple and the bread cubes.

3. Transfer to prepared baking dish. Bake for 1 hour (allow to sit for about 5-10 minutes to firm up).

Serves 6

PERFECT ACCOMPANIMENT TO HAM

If you are like me, I never know what starch side dish to serve with ham. Well this ham stuffing is exactly the right side dish. My mom always served this with ham on Easter and we always loved it. I have shared this recipe with many who now have it in the repertoire of recipes.

Here is the lovely Betty Martin Egofske (a.k.a., MOM) with the prepared Ham Stuffing. When we were growing up Mom loved to entertain and she did it in style! Mom taught all of us five children that holidays meant the dining room was all decked out with white table-cloth, china, sterling silver, Waterford crystal and candles. And that made me love to entertain too! Mom and her husband George are active, fun people who love to dine out, laugh and see friends and family. Never a dull moment for them. They live in Frankfort, IL but spend the winters in Marco Island, FL.

CORN PUDDING (ON STERIODS)

2 cans whole kernel corn, drained

1/2 cup heavy whipping cream

2 sticks butter, melted and cooled

1 16 ounce package sour cream

2 eggs, beaten

1 package Jiffy Corn Muffin mix.

1. Set oven to 350 degrees F. Grease a 9-inch baking pan. Mix eggs, butter, sour cream, corn, whipping cream and cornbread mix.

2. Bake about one hour at 350 degrees until the top is crispy and brown.

   Serves 6—8

VERY VERSATILE

This recipe goes great with any entrée from barbequed ribs to Tex-Mex to steak or with your favorite chicken dish. Sara Levy-Buehner has taken the traditional corn pudding recipe and improved it with the addition of even more of our favorite ingredients.

This can be doubled and cooked in a 13 X 9 inch pan. For a spicier dish, add canned or fresh jalapeno peppers.

Here's the beautiful and talented Sara Levy Buehner along with a picture of her famous corn pudding. Not only is Sara a fabulous friend, she is also my official fashion consultant (I.e., she co-founded the Fashion Code), my interior decorator (i.e., she single handedly decorated my living and family rooms) and an wonderful hostess, mother of Zach and wife of Jim. Sara grew up in the Chicago area and now lives in Rancho Santa Fe.

DESSERTS AND BREADS

"Let them eat cake."

— Marie Antoinette

- ♥ BEST EVER POTATO CHIP COOKIES

- ♥ PINEAPPLE UPSIDE DOWN CAKE

- ♥ TEXAS SHEET CAKE

- ♥ BOURBON BALLS

- ♥ BANANA CAKE

- ♥ PUMPKIN SQUARES

- ♥ OATMEAL BUTTERSCOTCH CRAISIN COOKIES

- ♥ MONKEY BREAD

- ♥ TOLL HOUSE COOKIES

- ♥ PEACH GALETTE

- ♥ LAZY CAKE COOKIES

- ♥ ITALIAN BREAD ROLLS AND HOMEMADE BUTTER

BEST EVER POTATO CHIP COOKIES

1 pound butter, softened

1 cup sugar

3 cups Swan flour

1/2 cup rice flour

1/2 teaspoon baking powder

1/2 teaspoon baking soda

1 1/2 teaspoons vanilla

1 cup crushed potato chips

1 cup crushed walnuts

1. Cream together butter, sugar and vanilla. In another bowl mix flours, baking soda and baking powder. Add flour mixture to creamed butter. Add chips and walnuts. Cover and chill in refrigerator for at least two hours.

2. Shape into 2 inch crescents and place onto ungreased pan. Bake at 325 degrees preheated oven for 16 to 20 minutes. When cooled sprinkle with confectioners sugar.

A MARRIAGE OF MY TWO FAVORITE FOODS

Potato chips and cookies are my favorite junk foods. That's why I was so happy to get this recipe from my oldest friend, Rita Zajac.. These cookies are light and crunchy and delicious.

Here is the beautiful and talented Rita Zajac holding the best ever potato chip cookies, right out of the oven. Rita and I have been friends since high school. When we got together recently in San Diego for the first time in many years, the time melted away and it was as if we were back in high school just hanging out. After her husband Joe died suddenly when her two boys were very young, Rita raised them on her own while working full-time as an ICU nurse. Rita is a warm, wonderful person who is kind, empathetic and always makes me laugh out loud.

PINEAPPLE UPSIDE DOWN CAKE

2 1/2 cups flour

1 tablespoon baking powder

1 teaspoon salt

2 cups sugar

1 stick (8 ounces) unsalted butter, softened

1/4 cup vegetable shortening

1 1/2 cups milk

2 large eggs

2 teaspoons vanilla extract

1 20-ounce can sliced pineapple

2 tablespoons pineapple juice reserved

1 1/3 cups packed light brown sugar

Maraschino cherries

1. Preheat the oven to 350 degrees.

2. Make the cake batter: Combine the flour, baking powder, salt, granulated sugar, 1/2 stick butter, the shortening, milk, eggs, vanilla and 2 tablespoons pineapple juice in a large bowl. Beat with a mixer on medium speed until well combined.

3. Melt the remaining 1/2 stick butter in a 12-inch cast-iron skillet over medium heat and coat the skillet. Sprinkle the brown sugar over the butter, making sure it's evenly distributed. Do not stir. When the sugar dissolves, remove from the heat and layer the pineapple slices over the top. Place maraschino cherries in the centers of the pineapple slices.

4. Pour the cake batter evenly over the pineapple slices and gently spread to even out the top.

5. Bake the cake 30 to 40 minutes until a toothpick inserted into the center comes out clean.

6. Immediately run a knife around the edge of the cake, then put a plate upside down on top of the skillet. Invert the skillet so the cake is turned onto the plate. It should come out pretty easily. Let cool slightly before cutting into wedges. It's best served warm, but also good cooled.

Serves 8

AN OLDIE BUT GOODIE

Pineapple upside down cake was the favorite of our father, Bob Martin. My grandmother, Isabel Martin, used to make this dessert. The crunchy top of pineapples and cherries is the perfect top to this moist cake.

Here is my fantastic sister Susan Fox along with a picture of her famous upside down cake. Sue lives outside of Indianapolis and is a director in R&D at Eli Lilly & Company, where she leads a team to develops oncology drugs. A registered nurse by education, Sue worked many years as an oncology research nurse before she moved to her current job. Sue is married to her college sweetheart Randy, and has two terrific grown children and two grandchildren. In her spare time, Sue paints and volunteers and has many friends.

TEXAS SHEET CAKE

Cake

1 cup butter

1 cup water

1/4 cup cocoa

2 cups sugar

2 cups flour

1/8 teaspoon salt

2 eggs

1 teaspoon baking soda

1/2 cup sour cream

1 teaspoon vanilla

Frosting

1/2 cup butter

1/4 cup cocoa

1/4 cup plus 2 tablespoons milk

1 box confectioners' sugar, sifted (4 1/4 cups sifted

1/2 teaspoon vanilla

1/2 cup chopped pecans (optional)

Cake

1. Combine 1 cup butter, water, and 1/4 cup cocoa in saucepan over medium heat. Heat until butter melts. Add sugar, flour, salt, eggs, soda, sour cream, and 1 teaspoon of vanilla. Mix well.

2. Pour into 15 X 10 X 1 inch greased jelly roll pan.

3. Bake at 350 degrees for about 20 minutes, or until a toothpick inserted in the center comes out clean.

Frosting

1. Combine 1/2 cup butter, 1/4 cup of cocoa, and milk in a saucepan. Bring to a boil. Add the confectioners' sugar and 1/2 teaspoon of vanilla and mix well with an electric mixer

2. Stir in pecans, if using, and pour over the cake. Sprinkle some pecans over the frosting if desired.

   Serves a crowd

A FAMILY FAVORITE

Julia Egofske has carried on the Egofske family tradition of making Texas Sheet cake for every family party, just like her grandmother, Josephine Egofske. I can see why this is a staple because it is so delicious and perfect for a crowd!

Here's a picture of the fabulous Julia Egofske, our niece, along with a picture of one of her specialties — Texas Sheet Cake. Julia just graduated from University of Michigan and is now working in clinical studies at a Chicago Pharmaceutical company. In her spare time, Julia runs marathons and bakes Texas sheet cake and brownies and has many friends. We all enjoy Julia's engaging and interesting personality. She is a joy.

BOURBON BALLS

1/2 cup bourbon

1 1/2 tablespoons white corn syrup

1 cup finely rolled vanilla wafers

1 cup pecans, finely chopped

2 tablespoons cocoa

1/4 cup confectioners sugar, plus some for dusting hands and coating balls

1. Mix bourbon and syrup. Add remaining ingredients. Dust hands with confectioners' sugar. Make balls the size of walnuts and roll in sugar.

2. Store in refrigerator between layers of waxed paper.

   Makes 24 balls.

DRUNKEN COOKIES!

I found this recipe in Grandma Burke's handwriting and it brought back so many memories of Gram's marathon Christmas Cookie making each December. Her specialties were macaroons, Christmas wreath cookies and of course bourbon balls. She made tons of cookies that lasted through out the holiday season.

Here's a picture of our beloved grandmother, Betty Burke, along with her homemade bourbon balls. Gram loved making Christmas cookies and we loved helping her. Gram lived with us for twenty years and we have so many fond memories. Gram was so generous, kind and she had a marvelous sense of humor She was always cheerful and loved to laugh!

BANANA CAKE

3/4 cup butter (6 ounces)

2 1/8 cups sugar (14 1/2 ounces)

3 large eggs

2 teaspoons vanilla

3 cups flour (15 ounces)

1 1/2 teaspoons baking soda

1/4 teaspoon salt

1 1/2 cups buttermilk

2 teaspoons lemon juice
1 1/2 cups mashed ripe bananas (approximately 5—14 ounces)

1. Preheat oven to 275°. Grease and flour a 9 x 13 pan.

2. In a small bowl, mix mashed banana with the lemon juice; set aside.

3. In a medium bowl, mix flour, baking soda and salt; set aside.

4. In a large bowl, cream 3/4 cup butter and 2 1/8 cups sugar until light and fluffy.

5. Beat in eggs, one at a time, then stir in 2 teaspoons vanilla.

6. Beat in the flour mixture alternately with the buttermilk.

7. Stir in banana mixture.

8. Pour batter into prepared pan and bake in preheated oven for one hour or until toothpick inserted in center comes out clean.

9. Remove from oven and place directly into the freezer for 45 minutes. This will make the cake very moist.

10. Frost with your favorite cream cheese frosting

   Serves a crowd

YOU WILL GO BANANAS

This cake is moist and delicious and well worth the effort. Serve as the ending to your special dinner or holiday party and your guests will love you.

Banana cake frosted with cream cheese frosting

PECAN PUMPKIN BUTTER DESSERT SQUARES

1 package yellow cake mix; set aside one cup

1/2 cup butter, melted

3 large eggs

1 jar of Muirhead Pecan Pumpkin butter (i.e., William Sonoma carries this product)

2 tablespoons milk

1 tablespoon flour

1/4 cup sugar

1/4 cup butter, softened

1 teaspoon cinnamon

1. Preheat oven to 350°. Divide yellow cake mix, placing all but one cup in a mixing bowl. Stir the melted butter and one egg into the cake mix. Press the mixture into the bottom of a greased 9 x 13 inch pan. Mix the jar of pumpkin butter with two eggs and milk. Pour over the cake mix.

2. Stir the reserved cup of cake mix with the flour, sugar, softened butter and cinnamon. Mix together until crumbly. Sprinkle over top of the pumpkin layer.

3. Bake for 35 to 40 minutes or until golde3n brown. Cool. Cut into 2 inch squares.

Makes 24 squares

PERFECT FALL DESSERT

When the kids were growing up, we were very fortunate to have Andrea ("Cookie") Erickson live with us as our professional nanny for eleven years. After she retired as our nanny, Cookie went on to become the manager of a Williams Sonoma store.

While working there, Cookie discovered this pecan square recipe and would always bring us a batch to celebrate the fall. Our daughter Kelly loves these pumpkin squares and when in college, she was the lucky recipient of pumpkin square care packages from Cookie.

Here's Cookie Erickson, along with a picture of her delectable pumpkin squares. Cookie lives in Lake Bluff, IL with her wife Elizabeth. When not working as a family manager/nanny for a very lucky family, Cookie loves to entertain, participate in her church community and have fun with Elizabeth. Cookie is a generous, sweet and always cheerful person who is a joy to be with.

OATMEAL BUTTERSCOTCH CHOCOLATE CRAISIN COOKIES

ALL OF OUR FAVORITE INGREDIENTS

This recipe transforms the traditional oatmeal raisin cookie into the perfect blend of butterscotch, white chocolate, cranberries and oatmeal.

3/4 cup shortening, soft

1 cup firmly packed brown sugar

1/2 cup granulated sugar

1 egg

1/4 cup water

1 teaspoon vanilla

1 cup sifted all-purpose flour

1 teaspoon salt

1/2 teaspoon baking soda

3 cups oats, uncooked

6-9 ounces butterscotch chips

6-9 ounces. white chocolate chips

2 cup dried cranberries

1. Beat shortening, sugars, egg, water and vanilla together until creamy. Stir together flour, salt and soda; add to creamed mixture, blend well. Stir in oats, chips, and cranberries.

2. Drop by teaspoonfuls onto greased cookie sheets. Bake in preheated moderate oven (350 degrees) for 12 to 15 minutes.

Makes 6 dozen

Here is the beautiful and talented Laura Wallis, who lives with her husband Eric and children Luke and Kate outside of Charlotte, NC. Laura is an amazing artist who works full-time as an art teacher . When not teaching or raising her two young children, Laura creates phenomenally beautiful painted silk scarves that she markets and sells. Laura has an hilarious sense of humor and spreads fun and happiness wherever she goes.

MONKEY BREAD

½ cup granulated sugar

1 teaspoon cinnamon

2 cans (16 oz. each) refrigerated buttermilk biscuits

1 cup firmly packed brown sugar

¾ cup butter melted

1. Heat oven to 350°F. Lightly grease 12-cup fluted tube pan with short-ening or cooking spray. In large -storage plastic food bag, mix granu-lated sugar and cinnamon.

2. Separate dough into 16 biscuits; cut each into quarters. Shake in bag to coat. Arrange in pan, adding walnuts and raisins among the biscuit pieces.

3. In small bowl, mix brown sugar and butter; pour over biscuit pieces.

4. Bake 28 to 32 minutes or until golden brown and no longer doughy in center. Cool in pan 10 minutes. Turn upside down onto serving plate; pull apart to serve. Serve warm.

HEAVENLY

This is it! The classic monkey bread recipe, oozing with warm caramel and cinnamon. Monkey bread is irresistible!

Here is the very handsome and intelli-gent Daniel Farrell, who is my dear neph-ew, along with a picture of Monkey Bread just out of the oven. Daniel attends St. Mary's College in California and is major-ing in Applied Mathematics. Daniel wired our house for sound, fixed our TV, beats me handily at backgammon, and has even taken my "driving school" online course for cash. (Don't tell anyone!)

TOLL HOUSE COOKIES

2 1/4 cups all-purpose flour

1 teaspoon baking soda

1 teaspoon salt

1 cup (2 sticks) butter, softened

3/4 cup granulated sugar

3/4 cup packed brown sugar

1 teaspoon vanilla extract

2 large eggs

2 cups (12-oz. pkg.) NESTLÉ® TOLL HOUSE® Semi-Sweet Chocolate Morsels

1 cup chopped nuts

1. Preheat oven to 375° F.

2. Combine flour, baking soda and salt in small bowl. Beat butter, granulated sugar, brown sugar and vanilla extract in large mixer bowl until creamy. Add eggs, one at a time, beating well after each addition. Gradually beat in flour mixture. Stir in morsels and nuts. Drop by rounded tablespoon onto ungreased baking sheets.

3. Bake for 9 to 11 minutes or until golden brown. Cool on baking sheets for 2 minutes; remove to wire racks to cool completely.

A LATE NIGHT SNACK

When I was a kid, many evenings around 9pm while we were all watching TV together in our family room in Olympia Fields, IL, my father Bob Martin would declare, "I'm hungry!" Mind you, we all would have eaten dinner 3 hours earlier, but we all chimed in and said, "We are hungry too!"

And Dad would proceed to order a pizza, make popcorn with butter or he would get out all of the ingredients and make Toll House cookies!!! All of us five kids would eat those cookies straight out of the oven...divine!

Here is my father, Bob Martin, along with a picture of his favorite cookies — Toll House! Dad worked for AMOCO for many years as head of International Tax. Dad inspired me to be an accountant because of his success. Dad raised us all to be good students and always kept the bar high. He had a great sense of humor and was very competitive when we played board and card games … which I have inherited. We miss you dad!!!

PEACH GALETTE

Filling

2 pounds frozen or fresh sliced, peeled and pitted peaches
1/2 cup granulated sugar
1/4 cup cornstarch
2 teaspoons ground coriander
1/2 teaspoon sea salt
2 tablespoons butter, diced and for dotting the filling

Galette Crust

1 3/4 cups all purpose flour
1 tablespoon sugar
1/2 teaspoon salt
3/4 cups cold butter, cut into cubes
3 tablespoons cold water

Egg Wash

1 large egg
1 tablespoon warm water

Almond Topping

1/2 cup sliced almonds
2 tablespoons turbinado or other coarse sugar

1. Add flour, sugar and salt to food processor. Pulse to mx ingredients. Add butter and pulse until pea size pieces appear. Add water and pulse until ball forms. Remove and knead slightly. Wrap in parchment or saran wrap for at least one hour to chill.

2. Remove the chilled dough from the refrigerator and roll it out into a 12 inch circle on a lightly floured surface. Transfer the crust to a parchment covered baking sheet and return to fridge.

3. Combine the sugar, cornstarch, coriander and salt in a bowl. Add the peach slices and using your hands toss all of the ingredients together.

4. Mound the fruit mixture in the middle of the chilled pastry circle, saving a small amount of juices from the mixture in the bowl until later. Gently spread the mixture out toward the edge of the pastry, leaving a two inch border all around.

5. Dot the surface of the galette with the diced butter. Fold the pastry border up over the filling, overlapping the edges and pressing the folds together every few inches. Whisk the egg yolk and water in a small jar, then use a pastry brush to brush the wash over the folded edges of the crust.

6. Bake at 425 degrees for 20 minutes, then reduce the oven temperature to 375 and back for another 25 minutes. Remove from oven.

7. Toss the sliced almonds with the reserved fruit mixture juice and spread evenly over the surface of the galette, then sprinkle the course sugar over the almonds and pastry crust.

8. Return the galette to the oven for 15 minutes until the fruit juices in the center are bubbling and almonds are brown. Cool for 30 minutes and serve with ice cream or whipped cream.

JUST PEACHY

What can be better than peaches, a delicious crust, almonds and sugar! This is a winning desert that we had for the first time at Nora and Alex Kaiser's house. I don't make deserts normally but I will make this one.

Here is the lovely Nora Kaiser along with a picture of her delicious peach galette. We first met Nora and her husband Alex when we lived in Long Grove, IL in the same sub-division and coincidentally now we are now neighbors again in Rancho Santa Fe, CA! Nora is the mother of four wonderful children and has it all. Nora always makes me laugh which is why she is so fun to be around.

LAZY CAKE COOKIES

1 box Yellow Cake Mix

2 eggs beaten

5 Tbsp. Melted Butter

2 Cups M & M's or Chocolate Chips

1. Mix together. Put in Greased 9 x 13 Pan Batter will be stiff. Use hands to flatten in pan.

2. Bake 350' for 20 minutes. Cut into bars when cool.

"HOMEMADE" COOKIES ON THE FLY

These cookies are so quick and so good! Add red and green M&Ms at Christmastime instead of chocolate chips for a very festive cookie.

Here's the fabulous Nancy Ryan, who is married to my father in law Larry Ryan, along with a picture of her prepared lazy cake cookies. Nancy is the mother of four terrific children and many grandchildren. Nancy lives in Naples, Florida and Oakbrook, IL. With Larry. Nancy worked as a guidance counselor at Trinity High School in River Forest, IL. Nancy has many friends, loves to entertain and is a blast to be around.

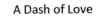

ITALIAN BREAD ROLLS AND HOMEMADE BUTTER

Italian Bread Rolls

1 cup water
1 ¼ tsp. salt
1 tsp. Sugar
3 cups bread floor
2-1/2 tsp. yeast

Homemade Butter

2 small containers heavy cream
One 2 liter. soda bottle, emptied and cleaned

Italian Bread Rolls

1. Set dry ingredients then wet ingredient on top in automated bread-maker. Set machine settings to bread dough only.
2. When cycle is completed, remove and place in large ceramic bowl with damp clean towel covering. Let rise until bread doubles in size and punch down. Let rise for a second time. When bread has risen to double its size, remove, add floor to flat board and configure into dinner rolls and long Italian bread rolls.
3. The Farrell family braids the bread as you would a hair braid. Coat with egg whites mixed with water and bake at 350 degrees for 25 minutes or until bread is sufficiently baked and browned on top.

Homemade Butter

1. Add the 2 containers of heavy cream to the soda bottle and shake and shake and shake more. The cream will first become frothy and then will turn into whipping cream. Continue to shake until a solid mass forms and butter milk separates. This may take anywhere from 30 minutes to 3 hours.
2. Cut the plastic bottle and remove the butter. Add butter to a butter mold or glass/ ceramic dish and refrigerate. Salt can be added after the butter is made.

CHURN BUTTER JUST LIKE THE PILGRIMS

Jay Farrell, my brother in law, makes these Italian bread rolls each Thanksgiving. We participate in the preparation and of course in eating these delectable little rolls.

We all take turns shaking the butter so that it is done in time for Thanksgiving dinner. It is miraculous to see the transformation of the cream into butter — just like the pilgrims!

Here is my smart and handsome brother-in-law ,Dr. Jay Farrell, along with a picture of his Italian bread rolls. Jay is a professor of electrical engineering at University of California at Riverside and is president of the Institute of Electronics and Electrical Engineers. Jay is an avid cycler and master sailor. Jay and my sister Theresa (his wife) split their time between their homes in Riverside and Long Beach, CA. They and have two grown children — Sarah and Daniel.

Here are the ladies from Royal Melbourne (our former neighborhood in Long Grove, Illinois) who prepared many of the recipes for this cookbook in their Long Grove "test kitchens." They brought their dishes to Joan Delott's Oscar party in March 2014 where they shared them and took photographs for this cookbook. Thank you chefs!

Roseann Bryne
- ♥ Luxembourg Salad
- ♥ Shrimp Ceviche with Chips

Mary Pacchini
- ♥ Asian Coleslaw
- ♥ Cream of Wild Mushroom Soup

Carrie McConachie
- ♥ Green Beans
- ♥ Mushroom Risotto

Cathy Hammer
- ♥ Curried Chicken Salad

Gail Nelson
- ♥ Gratinee of Cauliflower

Theresa Brandt
- ♥ Chili with Beans

Lyn Crosby
- ♥ Chicken Tetrazzini

Mariette Kaplan
- ♥ Lemon Chicken
- ♥ Perfect Cranberry Sauce

Jennifer Uremovich
- ♥ Chicken Vesuvio
- ♥ Fresh Broccoli Salad

Joy Kruswyk
- ♥ Spinach Casserole

Kristine Clark
- ♥ Sweet Potato Praline

Joan Delott
- ♥ Perfect Boiled Shrim
- ♥ Braised Kale with Bacon

Vicki Peterson
- ♥ Perfect Scrambled Eggs
- ♥ Torta Rustica

Maureen Sexton
- ♥ Lobster Bisque
- ♥ Broccoli Watercress Soup

Bridget Sevcik
- ♥ Tuna Niçoise Salad

Rosy Hugener
- ♥ Famous Guacamole
- ♥ Chicken and Shrimp Gumbo

Joanne Balogh
- ♥ Asparagus and Blue Cheese Salad

Sara Martinez
- ♥ Slow-Roasted Filet of Beef
- ♥ Mustard Horseradish Sauce

Nanette Kelley
- ♥ Thanksgiving Stuffing

Kathy Fanning
- ♥ Cajun Shrimp

Sharon Taylor
- ♥ Blender Bearnaise Sauce
- ♥ Grilled Shishito Peppers

Cari Sherer
- ♥ Holiday Pineapple Stuffing